Fascist Eagle
Italy's Air Marshal Italo Balbo

Particular thanks are due my parents (pictured here) for their help during the preparation of this book, Mildred and Philip J. Sgroi, Sr.

Fascist Eagle
Italy's Air Marshal Italo Balbo

By Blaine Taylor

Air Marshal Italo Balbo is pictured here on the patio of the Berghof with Hitler, Ritter von Schoberth and SS-Obergruppenführer Schaub during his 1936 visit. PREVIOUSLY UNPUBLISHED PHOTO FROM THE HEINRICH HOFFMANN ALBUMS IN THE U.S. NATIONAL ARCHIVES, COLLEGE PARK, MD

Pictorial Histories Publishing Company, Inc.
Missoula, Montana

LIBRARY OF CONGRESS
CATALOG CARD NUMBER 96-67018

ISBN 1-57510-012-6

First Printing: July 1996

Printed in the USA

The following authors and publishers have generously given permission to use extended quotations from copyrighted works. From *Italo Balbo: A Fascist Life*, by Claudio G. Segrè. Copyright 1987 by University of California Press, Berkeley. Reprinted by permission of the author. From *Regia Aeronautica: A Pictorial History of the Italian Air Force, 1940-43*, by Christopher Shores. Copyright 1976 by Squadron/ Signal Publications. Reprinted by permission of the publisher.

The author also wishes to acknowledge the technical assistance of Stan Piet of the Glenn L. Martin Aviation Museum, Inc. of Middle River, MD in the compilation of the photography for Chapter Nine. Special thanks to my friend and mentor, Mrs. Suzanne Sullivan, of Towson, MD.

Typography: Leslie Maricelli, Missoula, MT
Text Layout: Stan Cohen, Missoula, MT
Cover Design: Mike Egeler, Missoula, MT
Cover Artwork: Jim Farmer, Glendora, CA
Editing: Candace Chenoweth, Clarkston, WA

PICTORIAL HISTORIES PUBLISHING COMPANY, INC.
713 South Third Street West, Missoula, Montana 59801

Introduction

This is my second biography for Pictorial Histories Publishing Company, Inc. The first, *Guarding the Führer* in 1993, was an attempt to discover how SS Gen. Sepp Dietrich became one of Europe's premier political soldiers before the Second World War and top military commanders in the field during it. This effort, too, concerns an equally colorful, flamboyant and compelling character in the person of Italian aviator, aerial pioneer, model Fascist and Air Marshal Italo Balbo (1896-1940).

This year, then—1996—marks the Centennial of Balbo's birth, the same as that of my maternal grandmother, who died in 1994 at age 97. Balbo, too, might have lived an equally long life but for the tragic air crash that claimed it, alá fellow aviator Wiley Post. Balbo died at the young age of 44, two years older than Robert F. Kennedy and two younger than John F. Kennedy. As I write these lines, I am 49 about to turn 50, so I see the Air Marshal of the Aeronautica in somewhat my own life terms.

Like myself and Sepp Dietrich also, a good deal of Balbo's career was spent fighting Communism, one of the underpinnings of the entire Italian Fascist movement that propelled Benito Mussolini to power in 1922. Balbo, as one of the planners and executors of this movement and the vaunted March on Rome, was a mainstay behind both Fascism as a creed and the Duce (Leader) as a man. At a time when the late dictator's granddaughter holds his own former seat in the Italian Parliament in Rome, and a street there has just been named in honor of Fascist Minister Guiseppi Bottai, promulgator of the 1938 anti-Jewish laws, it may be well for us all—Italians and non-Italians alike—to consider the message of the life and times of Italo Balbo anew, for a better understanding of our own day as well as of his era.

This is my first book on Italian Fascism, but shall not be my last, as I plan follow-up volumes on Mussolini's foreign wars seen as a whole, Italy's place in the disastrous Axis Pact partnership with Nazi Germany that toppled both regimes and, possibly, a look at the foreign policy initiatives crafted by the ill-starred Duce in concert with his doomed son-in-law, Count Galeazzo Ciano.

This, then, is the first of those efforts. I came to the person of Italo Balbo by way of his German aerial counterpart, Luftwaffe commander and founder, Reich Marshal Hermann Göring, just as I came to the study of Mussolini via my initial interest in his German imitator, Adolf Hitler. Specifically, it was the many previously unpublished photographs of Balbo I discovered in the personal albums of Göring in the Library of Congress in Washington, D.C., that led me to decide that an illustrated biography of this largely overlooked, formidable figure would be possible at last.

That goal has been achieved here, with the first-publication ever of most of these wonderful, unseen views of the vibrant Italian Air Marshal. Initially, the text was done as a series of articles for *Air Classics* magazine in America that were never published, just as, earlier, *Guarding the Führer* started out as a series for a proposed magazine entitled *Age of Hitler* that was based on one on which I worked in the late 1980s called *Age of Napoleon*.

References to Balbo abound in many biographies of Mussolini and other Fascist Era personalities, as well as throughout the two Ciano diaries, but the real pioneer biographer in this uncharted field is a history professor at the University of Texas at Austin, Dr. Claudio G. Segré, whose 1987 work, *Italo Balbo: A Fascist Life*, did not get the widespread attention that this author feels it deserved. One of the best biographies of *any* World War II figure on either side, the Segré work should stand the test of time as *the* work on Balbo. I see my own, present effort as a *complimentary* volume.

As the father of the modern Italian Air Force—the Aeronautica—during the years 1926-33, Balbo attained the rank of the Duce's Air Marshal, and secured a place in the overall history of aviation worldwide as the initiator of four spectacular aerial cruises of flights of graceful Savoia-Marchetti flying boats—two across the Mediterranean, East and West—and another two across the Atlantic, North and South. Unique in their day, they have never been repeated, nor are they likely to be.

A hero in his own time, Balbo was portrayed as the man who helped bring the Duce to power, as well as the nation-building Fascist Governor-General of Italian Libya during 1933-40. He was sent there by a jealous Mussolini, whose pro-German policies he abhorred. Long before it became fashionable for the postwar revisionist historians after 1945, Marshal Balbo opposed the creation of the Italian Empire by conquering first Ethiopia and later Albania, was against Italian intervention in the Spanish Civil War that has been called a dress rehearsal for World War II, and was an outspoken and consistent opponent of the Mussolinian tilt toward Hitler that he predicted—correctly—would utterly destroy Fascism as a political movement and lay waste Italy herself. In all of this, Balbo was both seer and prophet.

Anti-German, he was also pro-Allied, and was well aware of the enormous Allied potential to blast the Axis to pieces; pro-Jewish, he was therefore, by definition, anti-Nazi. He was thus politically correct for our own day, as well as a loving husband and father who was intensely patriotic—in short, a man in whom Italians everywhere can still take justifiable pride.

If the Second World War had begun in 1929 instead of 1939, the Italian Air Force would have been among the best in the world, but it didn't, and such was Balbo's fate...

Blaine Taylor
Towson, MD

This book is dedicated to my friend, Judy Jones Spicer.

About the Author

Blaine Taylor was born in Washington, D.C. but has lived most of his life in Baltimore, Maryland. Today, he works in both cities.

This is his second book for Pictorial Histories. The first was *Guarding the Führer*, published in 1993.

During 1966-67, he served as a combat Military Policeman in South Vietnam as a member of the 199th Light Infantry Brigade where he was awarded twelve medals and decorations.

Taylor graduated with a BA degree in History and a minor in Political Science in 1972 from Towson State College, then launched a full-time career in journalism as Special Reporter, Copy Editor and Assistant to the Vice President-Treasurer of the *Afro-American Newspapers*, located in Baltimore, Washington and Richmond.

He has won six awards for his writing and editing.

Concurrent with his journalism career, Taylor has had a second career in public relations, including Director for the successful Bush-Quayle Republican Primary effort in Maryland.

During 1986-88, Taylor was Managing Editor/ Director of Research for Empire Press of Leesburg, VA, start-up Photo Consultant for the current *Time-Life Books'* series *The Third Reich* and East Coast Contributing Editor for Challenge Publications of Canoga Park, CA.

He is the author of the booklet *The Battle of North Point, 1814*, the special 50th anniversary commemorative issue on Pearl Harbor and *D-Day and Onward to Victory* for Starlog Press of New York.

His articles have appeared in *World War Investigator, Soldier of Fortune, Automotive News, VW Trends, Bulb Horn, Military, EMK: The Edward M. Kennedy Quarterly, Military History, World War II, Biblical History, Age of Napoleon, Sports History, America's Civil War, Great Battles, Vietnam, Wild West, War Classics, Sea Classics, Luftwaffe, Vietnam: Chronicles of War, Air Classics, Rail Classics* and *Second World War.*

Dedicated to Judy Jones Spicer, seen here with me in 1992. (Photo by Virginia Warfied, Towson, MD.)

Fascist Eagle

Contents

Balbo's flamboyant personality shines through in this dashing photograph.
PHOTO BY LUCCHETTI, FROM GIOVANNI TITTA ROSA'S *VITA DI BALBO*

The Duce's Air Marshal

"Italo Balbo: Large, Colorful,
and Fiercely Independent"
— Richard B. Lyttle

Italo Balbo, the Governor of Libya, was one Fascist leader who took pleasure in openly defying the anti-Semitic Aryan Manifesto promulgated by Benito Mussolini. Englishman Richard Collier describes such an occasion in *Duce! A Biography of Benito Mussolini*. It is July 1938.

"Without ceremony [Balbo] rammed his boot against the restaurant's revolving door. Into the hushed and opulent silence of the Ristorante Italia, Ferrara's most exclusive luncheon place, his guest passed first.

"The door spun to admit Balbo, his blue eyes flashing defiance. Deliberately, in full view of waiters and diners, he linked a comradely arm in his companion's. An embarrassed unease, punctuated by a subdued buzz of approval, swept through the room. In years past, the sight of the man taking his seat opposite Balbo would have been occasion for a task-force of waiters, headed by the maitre d'hôtel, to bow him to his table.

"Today, though, the restaurant staff were playing it by ear. As of July 14, 1938, two months after Hitler's visit to Rome, Balbo's guest, the handsome, saturnine Renzo Ravenna, Mayor of Ferrara, was a man apart. One among 57,000 Italian Jews, he stood proscribed by the new anti-Semitic Aryan Manifesto which Mussolini, in slavish admiration of Hitler, had just then promulgated.

"As Italo Balbo noisily set waiters scurrying, the diners exchanged meaningful glances. Plainly, there was truth in the rumors that had filtered from Rome to Ferrara: rumors which had it that many of Mussolini's old-time collaborators — among them General Emilio De Bono, Giacomo Acerbo, Luigi Federzoni, and Cesare Maria De Vecchi — had joined with Balbo to oppose the Duce's latest proof of uneasy vassalage."

Such action was vintage Balbo. No one, according to Collier, was more contemptuous than Balbo of the anti-Jewish laws. "On this anti-Semitic law, his scorn was so manifest as to reduce Mussolini to apoplectic fury," he writes. "'You seem,' Balbo lisped

maliciously, 'to be ready to black Germany's boots.' Shaking with anger after one such encounter, the Duce ground out, 'I won't guarantee the future of that man.'" Little wonder that rumors persist that the jealous, fearful Mussolini had Balbo murdered in 1940.

Italo Balbo was either respected or feared — or both — by his contemporaries in Fascist Italy and the Nazi Third Reich. "Large, colorful, and fiercely independent" are the words Richard B. Lyttle uses to characterize Balbo in his 1987 study, *Il Duce: The Rise and Fall of Benito Mussolini*. [Balbo] "radiated vitality and confidence. He was ambitious, and he could also be cruel."

Anthony Mockler concurs in his 1984 treatise, *Haile Selassie's War: The Italian-Ethiopian Campaign, 1935-41*: "It was Balbo, Mussolini's right-hand man and potential rival, who had caught the imagination of all Italy, and indeed of the world, by guiding a squadron of twelve flying boats across the Atlantic to a triumphal reception in both North and South America, where the Italian communities greeted with pride this outward sign of Italy's resurgence — the Duce had no partisans more devoted than those Italians who lived outside the reach of his laws."

Biographer Claudio Segrè's assessment in *Italo Balbo: A Fascist Life* is similar: "Pioneering aviator, Blackshirt leader, colonial governor, confidante and heir-apparent to Mussolini, the dashing and charismatic Italo Balbo exemplified the ideals of Fascist Italy during the 1920s and 1930s."

Italo Balbo was born June 5, 1896, the son of schoolmaster Camillo Balbo and Malvina Zuffi Balbo. An indifferent student, Italo nevertheless was well educated and a university graduate. Although his parents, sisters and brothers were all teachers, young Balbo became a writer. First and foremost, however, he was a man of action.

"He edited his own newspaper, the *Corriere Padano*...published a stream of books, articles and memoirs on subjects ranging from literary criticism to aerial warfare...Journalists, artists, and literary critics, as well as politicians and military men belonged to Balbo's entourage," reports Segrè.

The Balbo family discussed politics and world

events freely around the dinner table, with Papa Balbo maintaining one rule: there was to be no banging of fists. Young Italo chose republicanism as his mode of politics and even after he was appointed a Fascist minister in a royalist government, saw no reason to change this affiliation. Balbo became an avid outdoorsman, adventurer, marksman and hunter.

Flying also preoccupied Balbo. He was seven when the Wright brothers made their historic flight at Kitty Hawk in 1903 and thirteen when Bleriot made the first Channel Crossing in 1909. During the summer of 1913, Segrè reports, Balbo "wrote at length of his fascination with aircraft and his longing to perform great deeds in the sky...Like many young men of his generation, Balbo eagerly followed the air races and rallies promoted by the newspapers and other businesses. In September 1911, for instance, Italo, then fifteen, helped tend a signal fire for the Bologna-Venezia-Rimini-Bologna rally...Balbo also followed the meteoric careers of the flying heroes of the day, and mourned their deaths."

In July of 1913, Roberto Fabbri, a young man from Ferrara just Balbo's age, died in a crash at Malpensa airport in Milan. "Balbo paid tribute to his friend in a thirty-page pamphlet entitled *Roberto Fabbri, the Youngest Aviator in the World: Memories and Notes Compiled by His Friend Italo Balbo.*" The first half of the work was a paean of praise to his friend, notes Segrè, the second half an investigation of the circumstances of the crash. "Fabbri had his pilot's license and was soloing for the first time in an eighty-horsepower machine after training on a thirty-five-horsepower one," explains Segrè. "Balbo quoted excerpts from newspaper accounts of the accident that hinted that responsibility lay with the aircraft manufacturer, Caproni. In a long letter, also included, the company denied any responsibility and blamed the incident on Fabbri for doing stunts in the aircraft. In his conclusion Balbo sided against the newspapers and with his friend. He had occasion, Balbo wrote, to admire Fabbri's 'daring and not his rashness' and he did not believe in an accident caused by 'any carelessness.'"

Balbo married and, according to Segrè, had a long and happy marriage. "Inevitably, Donna Manù worried about whether he would return and often feared airplane crashes...He carried pictures of the women in his life—his wife, his mother, his daughters—in the cockpit with him on transatlantic flights. And he paid tribute to his wife in another way: the Savoia Marchetti 79 trimotor that he flew while

governor of Libya bore the civil registration marking 'I-MANU.'"

When the First World War began in 1914, Italy immediately declared her neutrality. Balbo believed war was necessary to defeat Prussian militarism and urged Italy to enter the war on the side of the Allies. That year Balbo met Benito Mussolini, a radical, Milan-based journalist and revolutionary agitator. He was eighteen; Mussolini, was thirty-one. "Balbo left no record of this first prewar meeting," notes Segrè. "The long and often tormented relationship between the two men began in earnest during the spring of 1921, when Balbo assumed the direction of the Ferrarese *fascio.*"

Balbo took an active part in pro-war rallies, often ending up in fist fights with the non-interventionists. Invited to speak at these rallies, he discovered a talent for organization and leadership. Balbo's first challenge of accepted authority, Segrè reports, came when he "led a group of high school and technical school students who confronted the police with the ultimatum, 'Either you declare war or we'll run you out of office.'"

Young Balbo and his friends later attempted to join a group of Garibaldini that was joining the French in their fight against the Germans, but were sent home by the border police. Finally, on May 24, 1915, the Kingdom of Italy declared war on Austria-Hungary and six months later Balbo was drafted with the class of 1896.

"He was accepted as a reserve officer candidate," writes Segrè. "He trained for five months at Modena, and on April 28, 1917, he was posted to the 8th Alpine Regiment. On May 1, he joined the Val Fella battalion and at last reached the Front." Soon Balbo was promoted to reserve second lieutenant. In mid-October he requested a transfer to the Aeronautica and left the battalion to begin pilot training at Turin.

"The official transfer is listed as October 22, 1917, two days before the Austro-German forces launched their devastating offensive that led to Caporetto," continues Segrè. "Whether Balbo ever began his training is unclear. His experiences must have been limited, for he did not receive his pilot's license for another decade."

Balbo was at home on leave when the Caporetto disaster occurred and his battalion was captured, leading detractors to claim that he had deserted. Segrè disagrees and notes that such a story has no confirmation in his military record, nor does it seem

Italy's air marshal gives his mother, Malvina Zuffi Balbo, an affectionate hug. Balbo was particularly close to his mother and sisters. Photo from G. Bucciante's *Vita Di Balbo*

Balbo poses with his family in 1940: from left, daughter Valeria, Balbo, son Paolo, wife Donna Manu and daughter Diuliana. Balbo's marriage, according to Claudio Segrè, was a happy one. "Inevitably Donna Manu worried about whether he would return and often feared airplane crashes...He carried pictures of the women in his life—his wife, his mother, his daughters— in the cockpit with him on his transatlantic flights, and he paid tribute to his wife in another way: the Savioa Marchetti 79 trimotor that he flew while Governor of Libya bore the civil registration marking 'I-MANU.'" Photo from Giuseppe Fanciulli's *L'Eroica Vita Di Balbo Narrata Ai Giovani*

characteristic of him...By November 10, Balbo was back at the front with the 8th Alpine Regiment."

Balbo finally saw action during July and August of 1918 against the Austrians, and led several patrols under enemy fire. On August 15, 1918, the Supreme Command's Daily War Bulletin mentions Lt. Balbo; Balbo was awarded a silver medal for valor. Balbo also took part in the October Battle of Vittorio Veneto, called the "Calvary of the Alpini" for the heavy losses sustained. "The goal of the operation was to cut off the Austrian armies in the mountains from those in the plain," states Segrè. "Balbo's Pieve di Cadore battalion was one of the units assigned to capture the Monte Grappan. The operation was a subsidiary one, but it proved to be the bloodiest of all...Of the 39,000 Italians dead and wounded at Vittorio Veneto, two-thirds met their fate on the Grappa."

During the fighting Balbo, like the other men, took shelter in the bomb craters, venturing out to haul in the wounded. He received his second silver medal for bravery. Then, at Monte Valderoa on October 31, 1918, Balbo commanded the first wave to break enemy resistance. "At Rasai, three kilometers from Feltre, on Balbo's own initiative his platoon broke up the enemy rear guard's resistance," writes Segrè. "In house-to-house fighting, Balbo and his men cleared the way for the main force to descend on Feltre...Balbo and his men entered the town...that evening. The attack on October 30 and the pursuit of the enemy troops into Feltre earned him a bronze medal."

"With a bronze and two silver medals, Balbo had a good war record," assesses Segrè. "True, as his critics point out, his outstanding deeds were confined primarily to the last two weeks of the war...Among Balbo's peers, Bottai saw more action and earned more medals; others, like Grandi, who made captain, concluded their World War I military careers at a higher rank. Nevertheless, Balbo did see combat—which Mussolini, for instance, did not—proved himself several times under fire and demonstrated his talents as a leader."

The war ended that November; Balbo remained in uniform until May 1920. At the same time he completed his university studies, began dating his future wife, and worked for a time in local government. In March of 1919 he entered the "Cesare Alfieri," Italy's traditional training ground for diplomats, politicians and civil servants.

The post-war political situation in Socialist Italy

was one of great agitation, as the following entry from Balbo's diary describes: "When I came back from the war, I, like so many others, hated politics and politicians, who—it seemed to me—had betrayed the hopes of the fighting men and had inflicted on Italy a shameful peace...Many at that time, even the most generous souls, turned toward nihilist communism, which offered a ready and more radical revolutionary program...It is certain, I believe, that without Mussolini, three-quarters of the Italian youth coming home from the trenches would have become Bolsheviks. They wanted a revolution at any cost."

Balbo was one of these angry young men. He edited a weekly military newspaper devoted to the Alpine troops with whom he had served and joined in street brawls against the Socialists, who denigrated the war and all those who had fought. As the post-war government was anti-veteran, at length Balbo found his way to the Fascist Party, which was made up of many vets like himself.

Notes Sir Ivone Kirkpatrick in *Mussolini: A Study in Power*: "In Ferrara, the most active and efficient center [of fascist squad organizations], the leader was Italo Balbo, who had served without particular distinction in the *Alpini* during the war and had taken a degree in political science at Florence University.

"He was not one of the early fascists and only joined the movement in 1920 when the landowners association decided to finance it and offered him the local secretaryship with an appropriate salary. He was then a thin, young man of revolutionary and anticlerical sentiments, with long, disheveled hair and a black musketeer beard.

"The year 1922 saw the fascist operations in the North assume a paramilitary character under the energetic leadership of Italo Balbo," continues Kirkpatrick. "He was a typical product of the war, a young man, then twenty-five years of age, who was unable to settle down to a humdrum peacetime existence."

To the fascist movement, the hotheaded Balbo brought students and others like himself. On the basis of his "extremely able leadership," write authors James Dugan and Laurence Lafore in *Days of Emperor and Clown: The Italo-Ethiopian War, 1935-36*, Balbo received the command of the fascist squads in Emilia, Romagna, Mantua, the Marches, Venice, the Trentino, Istria and Zara. As Kirkpatrick, too, notes, "The most important and the largest units in the fascist forces came under Balbo's direct control, and he...resolved to make active use of them.

As a young man, Balbo was a popular fascist leader. He is pictured here (top center, with cane) with his *squadristi* in Venice in 1921. PHOTO FROM G. BUCCIANTE'S *VITA DI BALBO*

An effective fascist leader, Balbo (right) personally takes part in ending a farm workers' strike outside his hometown of Ferrara. PHOTO FROM G. BUCCIANTE'S *VITA DI BALBO*

4

Fascist Eagle

"The first weeks of the year [1922] were spent in preparations and planning, and operations were confined to small-scale raids on the pattern of 1921, but by April Balbo was beginning to make his presence felt, to a point which threatened the authority of the State," continues Kirkpatrick. "For example, when the Minister of Agriculture visited the province of Ferrara, accompanied by the prefect of Bologna, Balbo with a party of fascists called on him to present a memorandum on problems of local agriculture.

"During the course of the interviews, Balbo took the prefect aside to inform him coolly that he proposed to kidnap the minister unless some fascists who had recently been arrested in Bologna were immediately released. The prefect assured him that the men had been arrested purely as a precautionary measure and undertook to set them free within two days. He was as good as his word.

"In May, Balbo organized his first major operation. At the end of April, the fascist trade unions in the province were alerted and told that if the government did not initiate local public works in order to diminish unemployment, there would be a demonstration of force at Ferrara and the invading detachments would not leave the town until the government had given way.

"On the appointed date—May 16, 1922—63,000 armed fascists appeared at the gate of Ferrara...The whole life of the city was paralyzed...The government had given way, and on the following day Balbo withdrew his victorious and elated culprits from Ferrara."

On May 29, 1922, Balbo again occupied Bologna with a force of 20,000 fascist militia to protest the recent killing of a Blackshirt. This time the local prefect would not back off, and fighting appeared possible. According to Kirkpatrick, the Duce, seeking at all costs to avoid a conflict with the Royal Italian Army, wrote to Balbo: "Dear Friend, it is necessary to terminate, for a period which will be very short, your magnificent action. The state has resolved to display for the first time ... its capacity to live and to resist. A pause is necessary. We must not exhaust our superb militia."

Balbo withdrew, but on July 26, 1922, occupied Ravenna as a reprisal for socialist attacks on fascists. Again the Duce ordered Balbo to withdraw. Asserts Kirkpatrick, "This reversal, for which Balbo blamed Mussolini, did not, however, cool his adventurous ardor." On August 3, 1922, in response to a request from the Parma *fascisti* that he occupy their city as well, Balbo called out the squads of Piacenza, Cremona, Mantua, Reggio Emilia, Modena, Bologna and Ferrara and entered Parma in force. This time firing broke out between the *fascisti* and the socialists.

The next night, after the local army general refused to intervene to keep order, a battle broke out with the Reds. Balbo then bluffed the army into declaring a state of siege and removing the Red barricades. Writes Kirkpatrick, "After two failures, he had won a resounding victory." There were now two governments in northern Italy: the real one operating from Rome and Balbo's. Meanwhile the Duce, in Kirkpatrick's words, was "leading the army from behind."

For the first—but not the last—time, Balbo and the Duce clashed. "Balbo bitterly resented his constant interference," explains Kirkpatrick, "and Bianchi was accordingly instructed to dispatch a letter in Mussolini's name designed to smooth Balbo's ruffled feathers." Read the letter, "It is ridiculous that you should doubt my complete, unconditional, unlimited, fraternal confidence in you."

Balbo had a tough, independent spirit and did not hide the fact that he feared no one, not even the all-powerful Duce. In *Il Duce: The Rise and Fall of Benito Mussolini*, Richard B. Lyttle summarizes the situation on the eve of the fascist march on Rome: "In Northern Italy [in 1922], the Blackshirts had established their own military lines of command. Various districts were commanded by...uncompromising leaders. The most active, and by far the most troublesome, was Italo Balbo, who ruled the Bologna District...Mussolini was embarrassed. His fellow deputies in parliament expected him to control Balbo. It was impossible. Mussolini could not even criticize the man publicly without rousing the anger of the Blackshirts."

Thus, prior to the March of Rome, Balbo was perhaps the Italian socialists and communists' greatest enemy. States Christopher Hibbert in *Benito Mussolini: A Biography,* "These *squadristi* obtained the support and admiration of thousands of Italians who were prepared to condone their methods in the belief that only by terrorizing their opponents, by making them salute the fascist flag as Italo Balbo did in Ferrara, by filling them with castor oil, even killing them, could the disease of international Bolshevism be wiped out...[They] were terrorists and murderers, too."

The situation in Italy continued to deteriorate as

the legal government in Rome increasingly lost power to the fascist party in the outlying provinces. On October 16, 1922, the Duce convened a top-secret meeting in Milan to decide whether to seize power by force. Balbo was present and, characteristically, wanted to act immediately, before the police and army could move against the fascists. Writes Kirkpatrick, "Mussolini said that he agreed with Balbo. Nevertheless, he refused to commit himself to an immediate decision."

Not surprisingly, the uprising that brought the fascists to power came to be a source of friction between Mussolini and Balbo. Mussolini took full credit and assigned only an advisory role to Balbo. Reads his autobiography: "We were on the eve of the historic March on the Eternal City. Having completed my survey and estimate of conditions in the provinces, having listened to the reports of the various chiefs of the Blackshirts, having selected the plans of action and having determined in a general way upon the most favorable moment, I called together in Florence the chiefs of the fascist movement and of the squads of action.

"There were Michele Bianchi, De Bono, Italo Balbo, Giurati and various others...At a fixed moment, the squads of action of all Italy were to be in arms. They would have to occupy the vital nerve centers—the cities, and the post offices, the prefectures, police headquarters, railroad stations, and military barracks.

"The political powers of our 'National Director-ate' were turned over to a military *quadrumvirate* [four men] of action in the persons of General De Bono, De Vecchi, Italo Balbo and Michele Bianchi. I presided over the *quadrumvirate* and I was the Duce [Leader], and had the ultimate responsibility for the work of the four men."

Balbo told a different story. "Balbo," writes Hibbert, "suggested that it was himself and Bianchi who advocated the March on Rome and that Mussolini was so cautious that it was considered necessary to tell him that the fascists would march on Rome whether Mussolini agreed or not." It was generally recognized, Hibbert believes, that Balbo was the most intelligent of the *quadrumvirs*.

Paolo Monelli writes in *Mussolini: The Intimate Life of a Demagogue* that Balbo asserted that he had selected the four men—including himself—and had pointedly not selected the Duce as one of them. Furthermore, when they met at Bordighera to organize the March on Rome, Balbo described Mussolini

as "unwilling to carry out the March on Rome until it was forced on him." According to Balbo, it was he and fellow firebrand Dino Grandi who, by threatening to go forward with the plan even without Mussolini's consent, sparked the March on Rome.

Laura Fermi gives this appraisal in *Mussolini*: "Balbo became a self-appointed general...The spirit of adventure dominated him. The sight of blood, of buildings set on fire by his fascist squads, the perpetuation of violence, elated him as no drug could have done. His feats were the test of his efficiency and a rehearsal for later exploits."

Although violence appeared to be Balbo's element, an August 1922 diary entry admits to fear. It was a terrifying night. Our passage was signaled with high columns of fire and smoke. The entire Romagnan plain all the way to the hills was subjected to the furious reprisals of the fascists, who were decided once and for all to put an end to the Red terror.

The famous poet Gabrielle D'Annunzio, who began flying at 52, was an early pre-Fascist ace and air hero of World War I. In January 1916 he almost lost his sight in a crash near Trieste. The following year—against medical advice—he resumed combat flights and "Led a series of three raids in a formation of more than 20 planes over the enemy port of Pola," asserts Laura Fermi in *Mussolini*, "on the southern coast of Istria, where the Austrian Fleet was at anchor." His squadron dropped "tons of bombs" despite enemy guns and searchlights. PHOTO FROM THE U.S. NATIONAL ARCHIVES, WASHINGTON, D.C.

On October 27 at 10:00 P.M., Italian Prime Minister Luigi Facta resigned. The next day, fearing a civil war that would topple him from his throne and discard the House of Savoy, as had been the fate of dynasties in Russia, Germany and Austria in the final two years of the First World War, King Victor Emmanuel III refused to sign a decree declaring a state of siege that would have brought the army into play against the fascists. That same day, the fascists marched on Rome. On October 28, the king asked Mussolini to form a fascist cabinet. The fascists had won political victory, and the Duce took the night train from Milan to Rome. It was a heady victory for thirty-eight-year-old Mussolini and twenty-five-year-old Balbo.

Mussolini claimed to have named Balbo (second from right) one of the fascist *quadrumvirs* [four leaders] just prior to the March on Rome in October 1922. Balbo maintained that he was self-appointed.
PHOTO FROM G. BUCCIANTE'S *VITA DI BALBO*

Fascist leaders rendezvous during the celebrated Fascist Party March on Rome, October 1922. Twenty-five-year-old Iron Beard Balbo, his red hair unkempt, appears fourth from right. Mussolini wears a sash across his chest and spats on his shoes (one of his trademarks). To the left of the Duce is *quadrumvir* Cesare Maria De Vecchi, a Piedmont landowner; at far right, in white goatee, is *quadrumvir* army general Emilio De Bono.
PHOTO FROM THE U.S. NATIONAL ARCHIVES, COLLEGE PARK, MD

Prophet of Air Power: Giulio Douhet (1869-1930)

Giulio Douhet was thirty-nine and a major when he witnessed French aviation in Rome in 1908. "Since the airplane is already capable of rising a few feet," he wrote later, "soon it will be able to rise thousands of feet and cover a distance of thousands of miles."

Notes David Nevin in his work *Architects of Air Power*: "What permitted him [Douhet] to see such prospects where others saw only the uncertain staggerings of a flimsy contraption no one can say; he had already been musing for three years about the application of this new device to warfare, and his ideas would trigger a titanic clash of prophecies that would polarize military thinking for decades."

"For many generations," explains Nevin, "the Douhet family had maintained a tradition of military service to the House of Savoy. The Battaglia family had an equally strong tradition of passionate journalism. It was not surprising, then, that the son born in 1869 to the elder Giulio Douhet and his wife Giacinta Battaglia became a career army officer who was also a talented poet and playwright and frequently a thorn in the side of his superiors.

"By 1909, the younger Giulio Douhet had become adept at presenting his ideas and cared not whom they might offend. He had written two significant books on the mechanization of war, an achievement that made him somewhat suspect in the minds of senior officers: men who were expert in the deployment of horse cavalry found him altogether too clever, too theoretical and too little interested in regular duty.

"Douhet was given command of a special motorized unit, but the high command was not interested in the ideas about the military uses of airplanes he was beginning to express; it had already decided that the future of military aviation lay with dirigibles. None of this deterred Douhet. He had seen only three airplanes...and he had never flown, but he had intuitively recognized the future of air power.

"He wrote an article for a military newspaper that was stunningly prophetic. In a few words he explained the nature of the new weapon. First, with a detailed and closely reasoned argument, he predicted that the air weapons of the future would be airplanes, not dirigibles. Then he wrote: 'To us who have until now been inexorably bound to the surface of the earth, it must seem that the sky, too, is to become another battlefield no less important than the battlefields on land and sea. For if there are nations that exist untouched by the sea, there are none that exist without the breath of air.'

"'Today we are fully aware of the importance of having command of the seas; soon command of the air will be equally important, for the advantage of aerial observation and the ability to see targets clearly can be fully exploited only when the enemy is compelled to remain earth-bound. The army and navy must recognize in the air force the birth of a third brother—younger, but none the less important, in the great military family.'

"In embryo form, the central concepts were all there: the quantum leap in their total war, implied in the idea that the air, bathing all nations equally, would become a battlefield extending far beyond front lines and national borders; the basic purpose of the new weapon, drawn from lessons learned at sea and summed up in the enduring phrase 'command of the air,' and the recognition of the crucial role of the air weapon in war, not as an adjunct to land and sea forces, but as a separate organization with a mission of its own."

"But the life of a prophet is not easy," continues Nevin. "Douhet's ideas brought no reaction from the Italian General Staff, although Italy did become the first nation to take the airplane to war. In 1910, the army purchased a few aircraft as an experiment. The next year Italy fell into a brief conflict with Turkey and invaded Libya, at that time a Turkish colony. After some hesitation, the Italian army sent along its nine-airplane flotilla.

"The world's first combat reconnaissance began at 6:19 A.M. on October 23, 1911, when Captain Carlo Piazza took off from Tripoli and flew along the road to Azizia. He was back at 7:20 A.M. with a report on enemy troop placements. The first bombing mission took place on November 1 when a pilot dropped four bombs on Turkish troops. Each was exploded by a grenade after the pilot pulled the pin with his teeth and dropped the four-pound package over the side. Early the next year, Captain Piazza borrowed a camera, took it aloft and originated aerial photographic reconnaissance. The air war came full circle when Turkish troops shot down an Italian plane with rifle fire.

"The army was sufficiently impressed by the achievements of its airplanes to form an aviation battalion. Douhet commanded this unit for a time, but soon ran afoul of his superiors again. Without authorization, he commissioned a friend, designer Gianni Caproni, to build a three-engined, 300-horse-power bomber that was years ahead of its time. Although the aircraft eventually tested successfully—the War Ministry was to send forty of them to the front during the first year of World War I—Douhet's unauthorized approval of the prototype gave his enemies the weapon they needed.

"Stung by his incessant criticisms and irritated by his single-minded advocacy of air power, they used this infraction as an excuse to remove him from command of the Aviation Battalion and post him to an infantry division. Douhet soon handed his foes another, more destructive weapon to use against him. A stinging memorandum in which he detailed military shortcomings and predicted disaster was made public after the outbreak of the Great War.

"This time he was court-martialed and imprisoned for a year. Soon after his release the very kind of catastrophe he had predicted occurred when the Austro-German forces broke the Italian line at Caporetto. The awful bloodletting that followed—there were 600,000 casualties—was the worst disaster in Italy's military history.

"Although exonerated by events, Douhet found that he still could not influence military planning as he wished. Eight months after his release from prison he resigned from active service and devoted himself to writing. It was then that Douhet produced the definitive book, *Command of the Air*, that assured his place in history as the first prophet of air power. Published in 1921, it was a detailed, carefully formulated set of theories for understanding, organizing and conducting the war of the future. He believed that improved firepower could stop any army and that therefore any future land battle would result in a stalemate precisely like the one that had characterized the recently ended World War I...Only the airplane, he argued, had the freedom to disregard the front lines, take the offensive and inflict total war on the enemy."

Italian Gen. Giulio Douhet was Balbo's mentor. In his 1921 book, *Command of the Air*, Douhet wrote: "A nation which has command of the air...can bomb the interior of an enemy's country so devastatingly that the physical and moral resistance of the people would also collapse...An aerial fleet capable of dumping hundreds of tons of bombs can easily be organized; therefore, the striking force and magnitude of an aerial offensive, considered from the standpoint of either material or moral significance, are far more effective than those of any other offensive yet known." Other disciples of Douhet included Germany's Hermann Göring, America's Carl "Tooey" Spaatz, and the U.K.'s "Bomber" Harris. PHOTO FROM THE U.S. NATIONAL ARCHIVES, COLLEGE PARK, MD

This formal, signed portrait of Balbo was taken during his reign as commander of the Fascist militia. Photo from the Caproni Museum Archive, Rome, Italy

Balbo's Rise to Power

"He was vain, of course, like many heroes, but it was a virile and agreeable type of vanity."

–Eugen Dollmann

On August 5, 1942, at his temporary Russian Front Headquarters in the Ukraine, Adolf Hitler entertains a special guest, the man he has placed in charge of the Mediterranean theater, Luftwaffe Field Marshal Albert Kesselring. The topic of discussion is the late Italian Air Marshal Italo Balbo, dead now over two years.

Asserts Hitler, "The death of Balbo was a great tragedy; there was a worthy successor of the Duce, a man who had...something of the Renaissance in him! A man whose name alone was worth something!...Balbo had the great advantage that he had equal influence with both party and armed forces, and it is an ironic fate that he should have been shot down by Italian anti-aircraft guns." (*Hitler's Secret Conversations, 1941-1944.*)

Dino Alfieri, the Italian Ambassador to Berlin, also mourned Balbo's death. Alfieri includes this passage in his memoirs, *Dictators Face to Face*: "Balbo enjoyed great popularity. A splendid figure of a man, strong and broad, he had regular, virile features, and his small mustache and d'Artagnan-like goatee gave him an air of jauntiness that was most attractive. He had wide, vivid blue eyes and a masterful gaze.

"Imperious yet courteous, stern yet generous, vivacious yet sensitive, he surrounded himself with an atmosphere of congeniality. He brought to his work a characteristic tenacity and enthusiasm which greatly assisted him in the realization of his plans and earned him the devotion of those who came into contact with him or were involved in his enterprises."

Not all in fascist Italy were Balbo fans, particularly not those at the top of the party's leadership structure. True, he was respected, but he also was feared as a potential rival to Italy's strongman, Benito Mussolini. After Balbo's death in 1940 the Duce reportedly said, "He was the only one capable of killing me."

Balbo was keenly aware of the Duce's feelings for him. Noted writer F. W. Deakin quotes Balbo in his book, *The Brutal Friendship: Mussolini, Hitler and the Fall of Italian Fascism*: "Nor would Mussolini allow even the outline of a rival personality to appear in his vicinity. As Italo Balbo once remarked, 'As soon as he sees too much light shining on us, he turns off the switch.'"

Mussolini's son-in-law, Italian Foreign Minister Count Galeazzo Ciano, especially feared that Balbo might succeed the Duce. In his diary entry for December 15, 1937, Ciano characterizes Balbo: "A poor intellect, large ambitions, completely treacherous, capable of anything—that is Balbo. We must keep an eye on him."

Yet when Balbo died in a mysterious air crash on June 28, 1940, even Ciano seemed distressed. "Balbo is dead. A tragic mistake has brought his end," he wrote the day after Balbo's death. "The anti-aircraft battery at Tobruk fired on his plane, mistaking it for an English plane, and brought it to the ground. The news saddened me very much. Balbo did not deserve this end. He was exuberant and restless, he loved life in all its manifestations. He had more dash than talent, vivacity than acumen. He was a decent fellow, and even in political clashes, in which his partisan temperament delighted, he never descended to dishonorable and questionable expedients. He did not desire war, and opposed it to the last, but once it had been decided, he spoke with me in the language of the faithful soldier and, if fate had not been against him, he was preparing to act with decision and daring. Balbo's memory will linger long among Italians because he was above all, a true Italian, with the great faults and great virtues of our race," Ciano concludes.

Whereas Mussolini committed to working within the framework of the Italian monarchy once the fascists were in power, other prominent fascists, including Balbo, remained strongly republican. This dichotomy created a troublesome situation for Mussolini. Writes Denis Mack Smith, "[The Duce's main problem was] the disorderly men of violence upon whom he had increasingly to rely as moderate opinion began to desert him."

On January 12, 1923, Mussolini took action. He dissolved all the armed squads and established in their stead the Voluntary Militia for National Secu-

Italian Ambassador to Berlin Dino Alfieri (left) chats with German Foreign Minister Joachim von Ribbentrop at the Italian embassy in 1940. In his postwar memoirs Alfieri wrote of Balbo: "His exceptional drive and powers of organization were revealed in every sphere of his activity. His first Atlantic flight, which filled the whole world with rapt admiration, and his work as a colonizer, which turned Libya into a truly model colony, were achievements which will survive the passing of the years because they have become a part of history. Both in Italy and abroad he enjoyed a wide and almost legendary renown. His romantic, chivalrous appearance made him the idol of the feminine element." PREVIOUSLY UNPUBLISHED PHOTO FROM THE VON RIBBENTROP ALBUMS IN THE U.S. NATIONAL ARCHIVES, COLLEGE PARK, MD rity. "This militia," states Laura Fermi, "absorbed and incorporated the dissolved fascist squads. These suddenly acquired a legal status, while any other fighting squads became illegal...The king accepted an unconstitutional army which was under Mussolini's direct control...Gen. Emilio De Bono was appointed commander-in-chief of the militia, and two other *quadrumviri*, Italo Balbo and Cesare Maria De Vecchi, were in its high command."

The young fascist regime faced a crisis in June 1924 when a prominent socialist deputy, Giacomo Matteotti—a renowned anti-fascist—suddenly disappeared. It developed that he had been kidnapped and murdered by a secret fascist organization called the Cheka, modeled, ironically, on the Soviet secret police. Asserts Fermi, "The Cheka took its orders from Mussolini himself...or from one of his more violent associates, Cesare Rossi, Italo Balbo, or Gen. Emilio De Bono."

In the wake of the resultant scandal, Mussolini feared the king and the army would overthrow the fledgling fascist dictatorship. According to Paolo Monelli in *Mussolini: The Intimate Life of a Demagogue*, the Duce almost lost his nerve, but Balbo did not. He, like others, advised the Duce to punish the actual murderers and forget it.

It was not so simple, as Mack Smith explains: "De Bono had been suspended as commandant of the militia because of his involvement in the Matteotti murder, and his successor, Italo Balbo, was now publicly implicated in the murder of the priest Don Minzoni and in many other brutal crimes in and around Ferrara. Such was the public outcry that Balbo resigned (from the militia) but Mussolini, who very possibly feared this man as his chief potential rival, gave him fulsome and public praise."

The opposition, on the other hand, levied serious allegations against Balbo in the press. Balbo rode out the storm, managed to maintain his seat in the party's ruling body, the Fascist Grand Council, and even continued to advocate violence against the regime's opponents. The opposition struck back with several attempts on Mussolini's life over the next few years. On October 26, 1926, a bullet punctured the Duce's tunic and ceremonial sash while he was in a car. "Within the hour," reports Collier, "grim-faced Italo Balbo, commandant-general of the militia, was reporting to Mussolini...The would-be assassin...had died within seconds of the shot—stabbed fourteen times by the berserk crowd."

Balbo, however, did more than stir up trouble.

He helped create the Royal Forest Militia and, early in 1926, began probing the Italian tourist industry as a way of bringing in much needed foreign currency. A trip to Libya in April convinced him of the value of colonizing Libya as a way to alleviate unemployment at home and that better air routes and planes would facilitate colonization. On November 6, 1926, Mussolini appointed Balbo undersecretary in the air ministry.

In *Italo Balbo: A Fascist Life*, Segrè assesses Italian aviation prior to 1926: "Flying, popular as it was becoming, also harmonized with the development of fascism as a movement and as an ideology. Fascism proclaimed itself to be a new and revolutionary political movement, a break with the past, a path to the future; so was aviation. Fascism exalted courage, youth, speed, power, heroism; so did flying. Hence, many ex-pilots joined the fascist movement after World War I. Finally, Mussolini sensed aviation's potential for propaganda. The wonders of fascism could literally be written in the skies.

"Because aviation developed so rapidly during the 1920s and 1930s, the Aeronautica acquired a reputation for being *the* fascist service [just as the Luftwaffe did for the Third Reich], the one that Mussolini created literally from the ground up. Naturally, Mussolini encouraged this view. Italy came out of World War I, he claimed, with five thousand aircraft at the ready, thousands of motors and spare parts, several thousand properly trained pilots, and a bureaucratic structure that was adequate to the organization. Yet, by the time he came to power in 1922, Mussolini declared, Italian military aviation had been reduced to a hundred obsolete aircraft, only a dozen properly trained pilots, a couple of flying schools, eigiht or ten wretched airfields, an unreliable meteorological service—and the same huge bureaucracy. The fault, of course, according to Mussolini, lay within the incompetent and corrupt post-war Liberal governments. Under their rule, unscrupulous businessmen speculated on surplus aircraft; peasants who lived adjacent to airfields freely cannibalized the planes. Wings and tails became the walls and roofs of chicken coops; fuselages were turned into firewood. Officials responsible for civil aviation wandered from the ministry of transport to the ministry of merchant marine to the ministry of war seeking a bureaucratic home."

"Mussolini was exaggerating, although how much it is difficult to say," contends Segrè. "Between 1919 and 1922, Italy, like the other European powers,

Balbo's chief rival for power within the Italian fascist party was the Duce's son-in-law, Foreign Minister Count Galeazzo Ciano, and Ciano's diary provides a fascinating account of their rivalry. Ciano wrote this excerpt on December 15, 1937: "I received Balbo and asked him whether it is true he is opposed to the policy of the Axis. Reluctantly he confirmed in all essentials he is. He says that he doesn't trust the Germans, that one day they will let us down, that they may well turn against us."
PREVIOUSLY UNPUBLISHED PHOTO FROM THE VON RIBBENTROP ALBUMS IN THE U.S. NATIONAL ARCHIVES, COLLEGE PARK, MD

Ciano (left) stands beside Nazi Gauleiter of Vienna, Baldur von Schirach. Ironically, Ciano was executed for treason against the Duce in 1944. Von Schirach, convicted as a war criminal at Nuremberg, served 20 years in prison. He was released in 1966 and died in 1974. PREVIOUSLY UNPUBLISHED PHOTO FROM THE VON RIBBENTROP ALBUMS IN THE U.S. NATIONAL ARCHIVES, COLLEGE PARK, MD

Dressed in air force blues, Italian Foreign Minister Count Galeazzo Ciano (center) gestures playfully toward German Foreign Minister Joachim von Ribbentrop. At left is the German Ambassador to Rome, Georg von Mackensen. Ciano flew bombing missions during the Ethiopian war from 1935-36. He belonged to the La Disperata squadron, the same squadron to which the Duce's two sons belonged.
PREVIOUSLY UNPUBLISHED PHOTO FROM THE VON RIBBENTROP ALBUMS IN THE U.S. NATIONAL ARCHIVES, COLLEGE PARK, MD

demobilized. The Aeronautica's squadrons were reduced from seventy to thirty-five, and the budget shrank from 600 million to 90 million annually. Estimates of ready aircraft in 1923 range from forty to as high as one thousand...Mussolini did expand the budget rapidly from 90 to 500 million lire annually. He also recognized the Aeronautica as an independent air arm, much as the British did with the RAF [Royal Air Force].

"However, Mussolini glossed over Liberal Italy's role as a pioneering air power. The Italians could claim the distinction of being the first nation to put airplanes to military use. The occasion was the Italo-Turkish War of 1911 when Italy wrested Libya...from the Ottoman Empire. During World War I...Italian aviation developed rapidly. Italy produced her share of aces and heroes such as Francesco Baracca and D'Annunzio, and she developed a fledgling aircraft industry. Italians pioneered such tactics as mass bombings in huge trimotor Caproni bombers. When the United States entered the war in 1917 American pilots, including Fiorello LaGuardia, the future Mayor of New York, trained in Italy under Italian instructors. Thus, Liberal Italy ranked among the most advanced of the air powers.

"Mussolini's example of denigrating his predecessors was not lost on Balbo. When he became undersecretary, he, too, claimed that he had inherited a disastrous situation and that Italy could not face a conflict with even a minor power. Of all the armed services, the air force should in theory be the best prepared, for it would be the first to enter combat at the outbreak of hostilities. On the contrary, according to Balbo, the Aeronautica was the least ready of the services. Balbo clearly had a vested interest in such a view: the worse the situation, the more he could justify requests for budget increases. Ironically, among the world's air powers, Italy ranked very high. Balbo's predecessor, Gen. Alberto Bonzani, claimed to have left approximately 800 ready aircraft and another 800 in reserve. According to one estimate in a parliamentary report of 1926, this would have made Italy the second most powerful air force in the world. Only France, with 1,500 aircraft and 4,000 in reserve, was more powerful. Great Britain and the United States, it was estimated, had only 700 ready aircraft and 700 in reserve. Since one-third of the French and British forces were dispersed in the colonies, Italy's air power appeared even more formidable. 'Italian aviation...holds a place in world aeronautics that is unsurpassed. The organization

and spirit of the Italian Air Force is making it admired by every nation in the world,' declared an American aviation magazine. In the hierarchy of air powers," asserts Segrè, "Italy was challenging the United States for second place after France."

"In May 1922," notes Segrè, "he [Balbo] tried to form a flying squadron of Blackshirts in Ferrara. When he became general of the militia, he flew a great deal around Italy and wrote in 1923, 'I believe that the future of Italy is in the sky.' In 1924, he was selected as the party's representative to look into the development of emergency landing fields throughout the country. After he founded the *Padano*, one of the paper's first projects was to sponsor a local aerial exhibit."

In May 1926 Balbo flew with Mussolini to Libya. "The trip," writes Segrè, "reaffirmed Balbo's position as 'one of the most fervent promoters' of flying in Italy. The *Padano* also contributed to Balbo's reputation as an aerial hero. When Balbo arrived in Ferrara by air, even though he had flown only as passenger, the paper described his face as 'glowing' from the excitement of watching the panorama unfold beneath the wings of the aircraft. Thus, even before his appointment to the Aeronautica, Balbo was known for being air-minded."

In spite of his reputation, Balbo did not earn his pilot's license until the spring of 1927. He was a competent, but not an exceptional, pilot. "Nevertheless, in Italy as elsewhere, the 'flying minister' image was popular and a pilot's license became an informal badge of office," states Segrè.

On November 6, 1926, Mussolini appointed Balbo undersecretary to the Aeronautica. "Mussolini's motives for appointing Balbo to the Aeronautica," says Segrè, "resembled those for appointing him to the ministry of national economy: a good dose of politics, with a dash of consideration for his qualifications."

"For Mussolini," continues Segrè, "Balbo was always a source of anxiety, a 'buried mine' that could explode at anytime. Yet he was one of fascism's most glamorous and competent leaders. Mussolini could never afford to dispense with him. Aviation suggested a promising outlet for Balbo's restless energies. Mussolini wanted fascism and flying to be intimately linked...From Mussolini's point of view, then, Balbo, with his reputation for action, courage and audacity, seemed a good appointment. As undersecretary, Balbo would stay busy; as minister, Mussolini believed he could keep him under control.

In practice, Balbo did as he pleased. What Mussolini failed to anticipate was that Balbo would take to the Aeronautica with as much enthusiasm as he did—or that the position would turn him into such a hero."

"In the Aeronautica," contends Segrè, "Balbo created his most enduring monument. All the other institutions that he headed—Blackshirts, militia, the colonial regime in Libya—perished with the fall of fascism. The Aeronautica remains. Yet, for political reasons, even today the Aeronautica acknowledges him as a founding father only with difficulty. For example, an official ministry pamphlet published for the Aeronautica's fiftieth anniversary in 1973 celebrated De Pinedo, Ferrarin, Del Prete, Nobile, Agello, and many other great pioneers of Italian aviation. Conspicuously missing from the list is Italo Balbo. In the massive air ministry building in Rome, one of Balbo's proudest achievements as minister, public tributes to him are muted. The most conspicuous one is over the entrance. There a marble inscription originally read, 'Built while Vittorio Emanuele III was king, duce Benito Mussolini, minister Italo Balbo.' Only Balbo's name has survived. A careful search also reveals his name on a column dedicated to Italian aviators who died in combat. The Aeronautica's undersecretaries still use his office today, but nowhere in the modest room is there any indication that it was once Balbo's."

"Balbo's seven years with the Regia Aeronautica were among the best of his life," writes Segrè. "First as undersecretary (1926-1929), then as minister (1929-1933), he was responsible for all phases of Italian aviation, military and civil. The position offered everything he loved: politics, adventure, glory, patriotism, showmanship, military service. 'Everyone knows how I loved [it] here,' he told his friends at the end of his term in 1933; 'I'm leaving my heart behind here...Naturally, I leave this house, this creation of mine, with death in my heart.'" Perhaps, as Segrè believes, Balbo came to enjoy the power and regal splendor of his position as governor of Libya. Be that as it may, he "continued to fly and he enthusiastically promoted aviation in the colony...in his heart—nothing ever replaced the Aeronautica."

"The years in the Aeronautica were critical to his personal development and to his reputation. His achievements as an aviator transformed him from a provincial Italian politician with a dubious Blackshirt past into an international celebrity. He joined Charles Lindbergh, Wiley Post, Amelia Earhart, Jean Mermoz, Antoine de Saint-Exupéry, Francesco De

Wearing the cap and overcoat of the Italian Air Force, Italy's Foreign Minister Count Galeazzo Ciano (right) is greeted by his German opposite number, Joachim von Ribbentrop, whom both he and the Duce hated. At left is Vienna Gauleiter (District Leader) Baldur von Schirach, head of the city where this 1940 meeting took place. Ciano noted in secret *Diary* entry for November 7, 1938, "Council of Ministers. Nothing particular. The Duce was annoyed at the trumpeting made by Balbo over the sending of colonists to Libya..." On the 28th he added, "Meeting about citizenship for the Arabs. A sharp altercation with Balbo and Starace because Balbo made remarks which sounded offensive about the Party's policy." Previously unpublished photo from the Von Ribbentrop albums in the U.S. National Archives, College Park, MD

Pinedo, Umberto Nobile, Wolfgang von Gronau and Charles Kingsford Smith as one of the great pioneers of aviation's 'golden age,' the late 1920s and early 1930s. Like the astronauts of the 1960s, Balbo in his day ranked among those who had 'the right stuff.' Unlike today's astronauts, who are brave, brilliant, superbly trained, but not always personally memorable, Balbo with his colorful personality and sense of showmanship left a vivid impression. Today's astronauts generally shun publicity. Balbo, in his dual role as minister and aviator, courted it. His long-distance flights promoted frantic celebrations wherever he touched down, Rome to Rio de Janeiro, Chicago to Odessa. His familiar goateed face appeared in advertisements for aviation products. The Marx brothers' film *Night at the Opera* celebrates him generically in a brief sequence that pokes fun at bearded Italian aviators. His very name became part of the flying fraternity's vocabulary, at least in English. A *Balbo* came to signify a 'large flight or formation of airplanes.'"

In his excellent book, *The Interpreter: Memoirs*, German author Eugen Dollmann agrees with this analysis of Italo Balbo's all-encompassing image and global fame. "I do not know if Italo Balbo means much to the modern reader, but his memory lives on intact and undiminished in the Republican Italy of today, having survived the war years and the fall of the Monarchy. Balbo the fascist took second place to Balbo the colonizer of North Africa and Balbo the daring transoceanic flier, whose exploits stirred the imagination of the world in 1928.

"His death in the skies above Tobruk on June 28, 1940, shortly after Italy's entry into the Second World War, is still shrouded in obscurity, but to a legend-loving people like the Italians, it has only enhanced the myth surrounding him. To me, who knew him for many years, he was that rare type, the congenial hero. He never bragged of his daring flight across the Atlantic with a squadron of seaplanes at a perilous time when aviation was technically unequal to such a hazardous venture.

"He was vain, of course, like many heroes, but it was a virile and agreeable type of vanity. The conquest of a beautiful woman—and his conquests were legion—meant quite as much to him as a storm in mid-Atlantic. He was a Teutophobe and Anglophile, and showed it plainly in a way which also demanded courage, since from 1936 onwards it was undesirable not to like the Germans."

Balbo (left) sets an example by standing at attention with is officers. He wears a Regia Aeronautica flight suit. Balbo formally received his air marshal's baton at Ferrara, his hometown, on December 20, 1933. He was 37. Claudio Segrè describes the ceremony: "When Balbo made his entrance...'delirium' swept through the audience of 3,000 packed in so tightly that 'not one more person could fit in'...An old peasant woman...made the presentation. The inscription on the baton read: 'To Italo Balbo—First Air Marshal—Ferrar—Proud Mother.' 'Visibly moved,' Balbo accepted the baton, then hugged the old woman. The crowd surged to its feet applauding wildly, while Balbo stood at attention." Photo from *Signal*, courtesy of George Peterson, National Capital Historic Sales, Springfield, VA

Marshals of the Empire and Fascist Party *Quadrumvirs* both, Balbo and de Bono (white goatee at right) review Italian Army tankers at Tripoli's Moccagatta Barracks in 1939. According to author Edwin P. Hoyt in his 1994 work, *Mussolini's Empire*, his anti-Semitic policy "Was very unpopular with the Italian people...including Italo Balbo, who had several close Jewish friends...and made a practice of meeting them in the most public of surroundings." PHOTO COURTESY ACHILLE RASTELLI

Marshals Balbo and de Bono (left) receive the Fascist dagger salute from Libyan Colonial paratroopers at Castel Benito in a 1939 inspection. According to author Edwin P. Hoyt in Mussolini's Empire, Balbo's death "Stopped matters cold in Libya," where the British Army soon defeated his successor, Marshal Rodolfo Graziani. Balbo was against the Axis Pact, "and hated the Germans." PHOTO COURTESY ACHILLE RASTELLI

Italo Balbo, Father of the Italian Air Force

> "First it is necessary to build a sporting air force, then one that is disciplined, and, finally, one that is militarily efficient."
> —Italo Balbo

Appointed undersecretary for air on November 6, 1926, Balbo immediately undertook a thorough, in-depth review of the service he had inherited from General Alberto Bonzani. "Bonzani's numbers [of ready aircraft] were optimistic," reports Segrè. A few days before he took office, Balbo declared that as of October 31, 1926, the number of ready aircraft totaled 551.

"After a few days of studying the records, Balbo reduced the number to 405 and then prepared an acid test," recounts Segrè. "He ordered all aircraft to take to the air on November 28. Fighters were to stay up for two and a half hours and all other aircraft for three hours. Only 200 completed the test, Balbo wrote to Mussolini, and most of them lacked armament and were not suitable for combat. Of the 405 originally declared ready, 335 took off, yet 104 did not complete the exercise, for various reasons. At the beginning of his term with the Aeronautica, then, Balbo could really count on only 300 aircraft." Concludes Segrè, "How many of them were combat ready is uncertain."

As Segrè notes, Balbo recognized that the number of aircraft was only one measure of the Aeronautica's efficiency. "The status of ground facilities, such as airports, was highly uncertain. Some offices and shops lacked electricity; others had no water. Meanwhile, rain poured into the leaky hangars. Flying suits were in short supply, as were spare parts, fuel, lubricants, ammunition and bombs."

There were other limitations. "Only one contract existed to provide explosives to the Aeronautica; delivery could not begin for two years, because the manufacturing plant had not yet been built," reports Segrè. A desperate letter from a young pilot to Balbo in June 1926, contained a catalogue of inadequacies and concluded with a plea to Balbo to correct these 'errors and horrors' and to 'electrify' the discouraged and despondent personnel."

Nor, as Segrè points out, was the new undersecretary responsible for the Aeronautica alone. "As minister of aviation, Balbo was responsible for *all* aspects of aviation's development, including commercial and general aviation. As a military man in a militaristic regime, however, he devoted most of his energies to developing Italy's military force."

Balbo initially assessed the Aeronautica as "nothing more than an office for propaganda...to promote air-mindedness." He planned, writes Segrè, "to build from the ground up." "Now," Balbo wrote, "it is necessary to begin building military aviation and its weaponry has not even been studied. First of all it is necessary to build a sporting air force, then one that is disciplined, and, finally, one that is militarily efficient."

"Balbo, of course, had no intention of returning to the days before World War I when flying was a sport for rich dilettantes," Segrè continues. "To Balbo the term *sporting* summed up the mentality and spirit of the new service. Like champion athletes, he wanted each of his men to give his best, to dare everything. He was also pointedly contrasting the Aeronautica's mentality with that of the established services. Unlike the 'sedentary,' traditional ways of the army and navy, the Aeronautica would be supple, athletic, open to new military techniques and strategies, to new training, technologies, and styles of warfare."

Money—or the lack of it—is the bane of all government agencies. In this sense, Balbo proved to be just another weeping bureaucrat. According to Segrè, Balbo's single greatest frustration as minister remained the Aeronautica's limited budget. "For four years in a row, the appropriation for aviation remained fixed at approximately 700 million lire (between $35-40 million pre-war dollars). Year after year, his voice brimful of sarcasm, frustration and fury, he pleaded for more funds. 'We cannot eternally use good will to make up such a large financial shortage,' he declared in his message of 1930. He had to balance being thrifty with his matériel against being thrifty with his personnel. 'It is a policy—let me tell you—that has me in anguish every day,' he told the Chamber in 1932. The only policy he was really allowed to carry out, he said, 'and here we do real miracles,' was that of personnel.

From the inception of his involvement with the Fascist party, Balbo routinely angered his nominal chief, Duce Benito Mussolini. Richard Collier relates this incident: "At Ferrara, Mussolini had angrily refused to walk down the carpet of captured Red flags that Italo Balbo had spread before him like a conqueror." In 1923, the miffed Duce forced Balbo and other top Fascists to resign their memberships in Freemasonry Lodges. In this photo note Balbo's pilot's wings over his left vest pocket. PREVIOUSLY UNPUBLISHED PHOTO FROM THE HEINRICH HOFFMANN ALBUMS IN THE U.S. NATIONAL ARCHIVES, COLLEGE PARK, MD

"Perorations in Parliament were only part of Balbo's campaign for more funds. He appealed directly to Mussolini. In a polite note in September 1927, Balbo asked the Duce to give the aviation budget 'the special treatment I have so often pleaded for'...In the interests of national defense, [Balbo said,] Italy should prepare to 'take command of the air even at the cost of reducing the power of the army and navy.'" Balbo's words were a familiar refrain heard in chancelleries throughout Europe and in the United States.

Where did Balbo allocate the Aeronautica's budget? "To understand what the 700-million-lire budget meant," writes Segrè, "it is useful to put it in comparative perspective. Balbo did so regularly when he addressed the Chamber of Deputies and contrasted the Aeronautica's budget with that of the other powers, especially France. 'We are moving among giants: giants in wealth, in finance, in raw materials, in technical and mechanical plants and equipment,' he told the deputies in 1928. The figures support him. In 1930, Italy's national income (400 billion lire) ranked from a quarter to a third of those of France (1,350 billion), England (1,650 billion) and Germany (1,450 billion), and one-sixteenth that of the United States (6,650 billion), according to an estimate used by the Army Chief of Staff, Federico Baistrocchi.

"Inevitably," asserts Segrè, "the Italian aviation budget reflected the nation's relative poverty. In equivalent life, the French budget (1,341 million) and the English budget (1,900 million) ranged from nearly two to two and a half times larger for 1928/29. Even worse, while the Italian budget remained fixed, those of the French and English increased sharply during the years of Balbo's ministry. In 1928, the English budget grew by 71 percent over the previous year, and in 1929 another 79 percent over 1927; the French increased their 1928 budget by 14 percent over the previous year, and in 1929 by 144 percent over 1927. By 1932, Balbo pointed out in frustration, the French budget had climbed to the equivalent of 3,252 million lire, or more than four times the Italian budget (754 million lire) for that year.

"Balbo not only wanted a larger budget in absolute terms, he also sought a larger share of Italy's defense pie. He wanted to match rival services as well as rival air powers. In his annual speeches before the Chamber, he reiterated his views on the Aeronautica's critical role in national defense. Again and again he pointed out Italy's vulnerability to air attack. A narrow peninsula with 4,000 kilometers of open coastline and a few strategic centers was peculiarly susceptible to aerial incursions, he argued—as did foreign military experts such as B. H. Liddell Hart. It is only necessary to draw a compass circle representing a distance of 300 to 400 kilometers—the range of a bomber—on a map from Ajaccio, Corsica or Ljubljana, Yugoslavia, to show how easily Italian industrial centers could be bombed, Balbo told the Deputies."

The alternative that Balbo proposed to the Chamber was "an efficient air force that could retaliate with a lightning stroke, perhaps even a decisive one. The air force was the most cost-effective of the services, he argued. The issue went beyond division of the budget. Italy's defense strategy and the structure of her armed forces, too, needed to be revised. The air force's 'real capacities' to contribute to the nation's defense had to be appreciated and to be seen in the general context of the nation's armed forces. On that day the budget issue would be definitively settled, Balbo declared in 1930.

"In his campaign for an equal share of the budget, Balbo alluded frequently to how the Aeronautica's appropriation compared with that of the army and navy and how this ratio compared to other countries. In Italy during the years that Balbo was minister, the Aeronautica's budget remained at about half of the navy's and a quarter of the army's...in France the defense budget was divided far more evenly among the services. France devoted about 22 percent of her military budget to aviation, and England devoted a little more than 17 percent...Balbo's supporters argued fruitlessly for a percentage that would equal that of France and would push the Italian appropriation over the 1,000-million-lire mark."

Were Balbo's arguments valid? "Naturally, Balbo's lamentations have to be taken with a grain of salt," responds Segrè. "He was right about the order of magnitude. In competing with France, Great Britain and the United States, Italy was jousting with giants. Yet, like any good service chief seeking a bigger budget, he had a vested interest in making things out to be worse than they were. Just how bad they really were is as difficult to determine today as it was then. Accounting practices varied enormously from country to country; nations exaggerated or underestimated their budgets as it suited them. Moreover, as everyone knows, it is easy to do tricks with statistics, and Balbo and his supporters conveniently picked those that would best make his case. For

Balbo (left) addresses a Regia Aeronautica officer during his visit to Germany in August 1938. Balbo's strong personality is described in this way by Claudio Segrè: "Balbo did not always live up to his own standards. When it came to demonstrating physical courage, to risking his life, few faulted him, and most people enjoyed his boyish charm. But there was another far more difficult side to him that friends and close collaborators had to deal with. The suave, cosmopolitan aviator and politician gave way to the provincial boor. To a faithful subordinate, for example, he might say with a malicious grin and his familiar slight lisp: 'How long have you been with me?' 'Ten years, Excellency!' 'Bravo! Now pull off my boots!'"
PREVIOUSLY UNPUBLISHED PHOTO FROM THE HERMANN GÖRING ALBUMS IN THE LIBRARY OF CONGRESS, WASHINGTON, D.C.

example, Balbo claimed that the British and French apportioned more of their defense budget than Italy did. That depended on the year. The Aeronautica's share of the total defense budget at 15.1 percent in 1932 was very close to that of the United States (15.2 percent), France (15.5 percent), and Great Britain (17.8 percent)."

Continues Segrè, "In depicting the Aeronautica's sad state, Balbo also argued as if Italy's case were unique. The reality, of course, was quite different. The inter-war period was difficult for all air forces. Economic depression, inter-service rivalries and anti-militarist sentiment among the public all contributed to reducing appropriations. Technological considerations also played their part. Battleships, artillery and rifles, for example, were expensive to design and develop, but they had a longer life span before they became obsolete. Aircraft, highly expensive to develop in the first place, quickly became outmoded. Maintenance and training exercises were also very high.

"Yet, like everything else, the question of development costs must be kept in context...Perhaps Balbo's budget was small, but aircraft at the time were not nearly as complex and expensive as they are today. Aviation was still considered a relatively cheap form of defense. In 1929, with rapidly rising costs, the price tag for a military aircraft ranged between 200,000 and 500,000 lire (about $15,000)...In the late 1920s and throughout the 1930s, small nations such as Poland, Yugoslavia and Czechoslovakia could afford to produce their own fighters.

"Finally, in presenting the Aeronautica's budget, Balbo ignored or downplayed where, on her 'shoe-string' budget, Italy really stood in contrast to the other air powers. Whether in terms of budget, number of first-line aircraft, or number of personnel, Italy ranked only fourth among the world's top powers, after France, Great Britain and the United States. Moreover, on a beer budget, Balbo managed to give Italy's Aeronautica a champagne reputation," concludes Segrè. "'The Italian Air Force of well over one hundred squadrons, smart and well-trained, appears to show more results for money spent than probably in another nation,' wrote a *New York Times* correspondent on November 29, 1929. In a world where the limits of air power were still not understood, where there was plenty of room for fantasy and for grand visions about the airplane as the ultimate weapon, Balbo did a remarkable job of filling in his material shortages with showmanship. In this he was

not unique, but he was unusually successful."

Nonetheless in 1933, when Balbo gave his last speech as air minister, he admitted that during his seven years as minister of aviation he never attained his goal of increasing the budget. "The fault," believes Segrè, "did not lie with him, although on occasion his salesmanship lapsed. During his 1927 budget speech, for example, he read his text in such a monotonous tone that a number of the deputies napped and Ciano gibed with delight that this was a wonderful example of *vol plané*, of flying with your motor off. To some degree the problem lay, as Balbo declared, in the nation's lack of 'air-mindedness.' The deputies, the public, and the military establishment could not or would not understand the issues involved. In France, he pointed out enviously, in addition to the minister and rapporteur, twenty-two speakers discussed the entire program for four consecutive days. In Italy, however, the newspapers preferred to concentrate on the sporting aspects of aviation, such as races and records, or resorted to sheer rhetoric in reporting Balbo's speeches. The rival army and navy regarded Balbo's requests with a jaundiced eye. [Army Marshal Pietro] Badoglio dismissed military aviation as nothing more than 'bluff.'"

Mussolini, as Segrè explains, walked a tightrope with respect to the Aeronautica and its budget. "In a dictatorship...the lack of the public's air-mindedness and the inter-service rivalries could have been overcome in the Aeronautica's favor. Mussolini chose not to intervene. Superficially, he appeared to be air-minded. He created the Aeronautica as a separate service in 1923...for the first four years of the Aeronautica's existence he supported a sevenfold increase in the aviation budget. Any further increases, however, at the expense of the army and navy would have alienated these senior services and eroded the basis of his political support. Mussolini maintained power by balancing the new fascist institutions such as the party and militia against established ones such as the bureaucracy and the armed forces. The party could not triumph over the state."

It was only between 1935 and 1940, after Mussolini took control of the Aeronautica away from Balbo, that the air ministry's budget grew at a faster rate than that of the other services. "These increases," writes Segrè, "reflected the 'special' appropriations prompted by Italy's involvement in Ethiopia and Spain. Without them the Aeronautica would have continued to lag behind the other services, and indeed the Aeronautica never came close to match-

August 11, 1938: A sprightly Balbo emerges from a swim at a beach in northern Germany. Balbo, according to Claudio Segrè, became obsessed with getting fat as he approached middle age. "Balbo's [friends] often had to put up with attending him while he took a bath. Invariably, he asked them if they thought he had put on weight. Then he would tell them: 'You suffer from the lamb's ill.' 'What?' 'Your belly's growing and your pecker's over the hill!'" Previously unpublished photo from the Hermann Göring albums in the Library of Congress, Washington, D.C.

This 1939 photo shows Mussolini at the wheel of a seaplane. Like Balbo, the Duce was a qualified pilot. It is reported, however, that Mussolini had such a serious accident while a student that anxious officials hid an instructor aboard his plane when he took his solo examination in 1921. Photo from the U.S. National Archives, College Park, MD

Father of the Italian Air Force

ing the army, which always claimed close to half the defense budget. On the other hand, the 'special' appropriations were a vindication of Balbo's policies. The Aeronautica had arrived as a legitimate military service with a major contribution to make to the war effort.''

In assessing Balbo's contribution to the Regia Aeronautica, it must be remembered that Balbo had one liability that other military ministers did not: the double-edged sword of his enormous popularity both at home and abroad. While Balbo's extraordinary transoceanic flights gave the Italian Air Force a golden reputation internationally, jealousy over these triumphs may have evoked unnecessarily harsh criticism of the Aeronautica and of Balbo.

Mussolini liked to be thought of as an activist dictator who did well at whatever sport he undertook—skiing, swimming, tennis, fencing, or flying. Here he shows off during Göring's visit to Rome in January 1937. Previously unpublished photo from the Hermann Göring albums in the Library of Congress, Washington, D.C.

Balbo Builds the Aeronautica, 1926-1933

"The myth of Italy as a major industrial air power was merely one of the many myths that the fascist regime fostered and to which Balbo contributed through his policies."
—Claudio Segrè

Balbo's views on the potential of aviation can be traced, in part, to those of the famous Italian theorist of air power, Giulio Douhet (1869-1930), with whom Balbo had many talks. "In the doctrines of the theorist," Segrè writes, "Balbo found powerful arguments for building the Aeronautica into an independent service that would have equal rank with the army and navy; in Douhet's ceaseless polemics about the value of air power, Balbo found a useful source of publicity."

Douhet believed air power to be the "ultimate weapon" against which there was no effective defense and called for the development of massive aerial fleets, a unified command, and strategic bombing training. "From Douhet's ideas Balbo chose those themes and doctrines that he found congenial and practical," explains Segrè. "He concentrated on three points. First, Balbo insisted that the Aeronautica had its own war to fight. The Aeronautica would cooperate with the other services as needed, but it would no longer be limited to serving as an auxiliary to the army and navy. In future wars, the role of the air force would be predominant, he predicted, and he believed that the development of aviation had revolutionized strategy and 'diminished the absolute value of the other forces.' Second, in Balbo's view, the Aeronautica should have a first-strike capability. Given Italy's strategic position, neither the army nor the navy could carry out this mission. Finally, as one who made a career out of organizing and leading masses, whether Blackshirts or colonists or aviators, Balbo naturally seized on Douhet's idea of aerial fleets. The day of the 'single machine fighting raids' as in World War I had ended, Balbo argued. He pictured 'hundreds and hundreds' of aircraft engaged in colossal battles among the clouds. Hence, there was a need for a 'completely new doctrine and technical strategy' for the Aeronautica that specifically recognized the characteristics and needs of aerial warfare."

"In developing a doctrine for the Aeronautica, Balbo was a pragmatist," notes Segrè. "In certain of his aerial cruises and maneuvers, like those of 1931, he experimented with Douhetian mass flights and exercises in strategic bombing. Yet he also supported those, like General Amedeo Mecozzi (1892-1971), who advocated tactical uses of air power. Both in his declarations and in his policies Balbo made it abundantly clear that he was not committed to either side. 'Neither of these theories can be altogether discarded...I think there is virtue in both,' he told an English newspaper while he was still undersecretary. As early as 1929, with Balbo's encouragement, the Aeronautica organized tactical units and practiced maneuvers based on Mecozzi's ideas."

"In general," continues Segrè, "Balbo developed a broader, more flexible vision of the potential of air power than Douhet did. For instance, Balbo never believed in the infallibility of Douhet's 'battle planes.' As William Mitchell, the great publicist of air power in the United States, observed on a visit to Italy, Balbo still allocated aircraft to defensive work. Nor did Balbo believe, as Douhet simplistically did, that military and civil aviation were interchangeable. Hence, he fought for more investment and development of military aircraft and for more modest appropriations for civil aviation. In addition to encouraging tactical uses of aircraft as Mecozzi suggested, Balbo foresaw the logistical capabilities of aircraft. For instance, in 1938 in Libya, he directed an exercise in which two hundred parachutists 'captured' an enemy airport. Reinforcements to secure the objective arrived by air in the form of one hundred transports carrying two thousand troops and equipment.

"Douhet's theories, then, served as a base from which Balbo expanded his own ideas and policies, but Balbo never acted as Douhet's devoted disciple. Neither Balbo nor Mussolini gave the theorist a position of authority...Balbo rarely mentioned Douhet as the inspiration for the Aeronautica's development. With monotonous regularity, that honor went to Mussolini."

In addition to theory, two practical factors influenced the design of military aircraft during the 1920s and early 1930s. "One," explains Segrè, "was simply the limitations of budget. With an eye to economy, air forces tried to keep down the number of specialized aircraft, to standardize as much as possible and to build all-purpose models. A second factor, at least in England, was the 'ten-year rule.' Under this assumption, an impending war would be clear at least a decade ahead of time. This meant that it was enough to build only a few advanced prototypes to keep up design and production facilities; there was no need to manufacture these aircraft in quantity. Production would begin when the war was well in sight. As a result of such assumptions and budget restrictions, by the early 1930s the major air powers were all admirably equipped to fight the air battles of World War I over again. The first-line aircraft were still the same as those that had proved successful in 1918—biplanes with fixed undercarriages and limited armament. No country had a clear advantage and no country had fallen behind. Thus," concludes Segrè, "a more recent Italian military historian, no admirer of Balbo or his policies, has concluded that, on the whole, the aircraft with which Balbo equipped the Aeronautica was certainly as good as, if not better than, those of the other air powers of the day.

"Two simple and compelling arguments support such a view. First, Italian aircraft during these years established an extraordinary number of records; second, Italy became an important manufacturer and exporter of aircraft beginning with Balbo's ministry and continuing through the early years of World War II. Between April 1, 1927, and November 1, 1939, Italians set 110 records, though some were held for only a short time. At the end of 1939, Italy still kept 36 of the 84 records established by the International Aeronautical Federation. Between 1937 and 1943, Italy exported aircraft to no fewer than thirty-nine countries. Many orders came from Latin America and Eastern Europe, but included were such air powers as Germany, Japan, England and the United States. Balbo did not always achieve everything that he claimed, but there is no evidence that he seriously neglected the Aeronautica's technical development. Balbo equipped his Aeronautica with aircraft that in their own day stood up favorably against their competition...

"The standard fighters under Balbo's ministry were the Fiat CR.20s and CR.30s and 32s. By 1931, Balbo had equipped his squadrons almost completely with CR.20s. This was a single-engine biplane of metal construction armed with four machine guns. Powered by a 400-horsepower Fiat A 20 engine, the CR.20 had a top speed of 250 kilometers per hour, a ceiling of 6,500 meters, and a range of two and a half hours. While it was not a particularly innovative or advanced design, the CR.20 had good flying characteristics and exceptional maneuverability which made it a reliable pursuit plane as well as a crowd-pleaser in aerial shows. From planning to prototype to production in those days was about a three-year cycle. The prototype of the CR.20 had been tested in September of 1926, shortly before Balbo took office. The CR.20's successors, the CR.30 and the CR.32, appeared in 1932 and 1933. The CR.32 became the most famous Italian fighter of the inter-war period...

"Critics have argued that, since their biplanes performed so well, the Italians were slow in developing the monoplanes that triumphed in World War II. This is probably overstating the case, and such an argument misrepresents the thinking in Balbo's day. In the early 1930s, the superiority of the monoplane over the biplane was not established. Most veteran fighter pilots felt that the key qualities of a fighter were rate of climb, speed, and maneuverability, with emphasis on extremely short radius turns. The monoplane, with its high wing loading, greater turning radius and greater speeds in takeoff and landing seemed to be seriously disadvantaged. The situation began to changed only after Balbo left the ministry. Messerschmitt, for example, began working on the Bf.109 in the summer of 1934...Similarly, R. J. Mitchell developed the Spitfire in 1934/1935 and the prototype flew for the first time only in March 1936.

"The bomber situation under Balbo was less satisfactory. In 1931 Balbo claimed in his annual message to the Chamber of Deputies that the bomber problem had been 'fully confronted,' that bombers made up the 'foundation' of the air armada, that 'worries over our inferiority had by now dissipated.' The reality was considerably different. Balbo's day bombers were mostly BR.2s and 3s, part of a long series of designs that had begun in 1919. Both the BR.2s and BR.3s were known for their records and distance flights. In 1931 a BR.3, together with a Fiat A.120 won the Prince Bibescu Cup with a flight of 710 miles at an average speed of 156.6 mph. Nevertheless, an aerial armada of these machines scarcely had the capability of dealing decisive blows to the enemy. The BR.2, for example, was a single-engine, two-place, open-cockpit wooden biplane that could deliver a half-ton (metric) bomb load over a 300-400 km range at a speed of about 240 km/h—about the same speed as a fighter. The night bombers, slower, and therefore theoretically unable to face fighters, were mostly Caproni Ca.73s and 74s. By 1931 these were being replaced by Ca.101 trimotors and twin-engine Ca.102s, aircraft with a much greater range (1,000 km) but no greater speed.

Segrè continues: "Every specialized land plane had its counterpart in a seaplane, for Balbo's ministry coincided with the golden age of the seaplane. In those days, retractable landing gear had not been perfected; fixed ones buckled and broke. Landing fields were literally nothing more than that—open fields...Both military and commercial aviation in Balbo's day utilized a well-established institution: harbor and port facilities.

"The Aeronautica's standard bomber and recon-naissance seaplane under Balbo's ministry was an odd-looking twin-hulled flying boat that he made famous: the Savoia Marchetti SM.55. This unusual 'flying catamaran' became one of the most famous and best publicized aircraft of its day. As Balbo's critics point out, the SM.55 was an old design. It was first planned in 1923 and flew for the first time in 1925. Its ruggedness and dependability made it a favorite for long-distance record flights, and Balbo used it for three of his aerial cruises. A larger variant of the SM.55, the SM.66 was used as a fourteen-passenger flying boat on commercial runs between Rome and Tripoli or Alexandria. The SM.55 proved so durable that it was not withdrawn until 1939, when the Italian navy still had thirteen in service."

If the combat aircraft Balbo readied as minister were not inferior to those of the air powers, however, their quantity and availability were a different mat-ter. "In seven years," notes Segrè, "Balbo ordered 2,000 aircraft. This was actually fewer than the 2,300 that his predecessors, Bonzani and Finzi, had or-dered in the four years of their administration. The types of aircraft that Balbo ordered also differed. He contracted for about half as many military aircraft as his predecessors and many more planes for tourism, general aviation, and training. Nor could he meet his goals for expanding the number of squadrons. In 1930, for instance, he had funds enough to outfit only two-thirds of his squadrons with CR.20s; the rest had to wait until the following year. In 1932 he noted that lack of funds prevented him from completing his three-year program. It is no surprise that he never came close to his 'wish list'—a total of 3,600 aircraft, including auxiliary forces for the army and navy, for which he estimated he needed a budget of 3 billion lire. 'The absurdity of this sum can save us from taking it into consideration,' he commented.

"During Balbo's ministry, Italy's aircraft indus-try, on which he relied to equip the Aeronautica, developed and expanded. Italy became a major ex-porter of aircraft. On the surface, these look like commendable achievements. Post-World War II, however, the Italian aircraft industry has come in for some harsh criticism. No one questions the skill and inventiveness of individual designers such as Celestino Rosatelli, Filippo Zappata, Giovanni Pegna, Mario Castoldi, Giuseppe Gabrielli, Alessandro Marchetti, or Gianni Caproni. Individually they produced air-craft that won races and prizes and established a host of records. The industry as a whole, however, failed to deliver, the critics argue. Despite a multitude of inducements—protective tariffs, subsidies, prizes—the major aircraft companies did not, on a regular basis, produce the equipment the Aeronautica needed," claims Segrè. "The classic example is the issue of engine design. While Italy built beautiful engines to set world speed records and win the Schneider Cup, the industry did not create a reliable 1,000 to 1,500 horsepower engine that could power fighters and bombers. As a result, the Italians had to rely on foreign engines or clumsy expedients such as trimotor bombers.

"According to the Aeronautica's semi-official historian, much of the responsibility lay with the ministry, which gave the industry directives that proved to be 'weak and uncertain and in many sectors erroneous.' In the relations between the ministry and the industry, the industrialists had the upper hand. If they did not receive as many contracts as they wished for, they raised the specter of unemployment, and the ministry satisfied them.

"Such a critique undoubtedly applies at least partially to the years of Balbo's ministry. However, it seems doubtful that stronger direction from the ministry would have resolved the Aeronautica's prob-lems. Such an argument ignores a larger question: should Italy have developed an aircraft industry in the first place? As one writer has argued, the myth of Italy as a major industrial air power was merely one of the many myths that the fascist regime fostered and to which Balbo contributed through his policies. He devoted much of his energy to building a national industry, independent in its designs, raw materials and financing. Since Italy's domestic market was far too small to absorb the national production, foreign sales became an absolute necessity. Italy needed to trade for raw materials or for hard currencies with

One of Balbo's many enemies within the Fascist party was Sec. Gen. Roberto Farinacci (second from right). A major bone of contention between the two was the anti-Semitic laws Mussolini proposed in the summer of 1938. Like Ciano and the Duce's two sons, Farinacci served as a bomber pilot in Ethiopia. PREVIOUSLY UNPUBLISHED PHOTO FROM THE VON RIBBENTROP ALBUMS IN THE U.S. NATIONAL ARDHIVES, COLLEGE PARK, MD

Mussolini (far left), Gen. Emilio De Bono (white goatee), and Balbo (center) march in a 1932 celebration of the 10th anniversary of the March on Rome. Balbo irritated De Bono to the extent that remarks such as these were common: "It took Italo Balbo, finding no chair at hand, to perch himself...on the edge of the Duce's desk. PHOTO FROM THE LIBRARY OF CONGRESS, WASHINGTON, D.C.

October 2, 1936: Hermann Göring (left) beams at the Italian and German air force officers gathered in his office. Italian Foreign Minister Count Galeazzo Ciano (center) toys with a model of an Italian bomber he has just presented to the minister. Also present are Luftwaffe organizer Gen. Erhard Milch (far right, with cigar) and Göring's liaison officer to Hitler, Gen. Karl Bodenschatz (center rear, near windowed doors). Ciano was ever-suspicious of Balbo and comments such as this were common in his diary: "Medici told me that he spoke to him [Crown Prince Umberto, heir to the Italian throne] frankly this morning on the subject of Balbo and opened his eyes to our Ferrarese friend's very dubious loyalty to the Monarchy. He praised my loyalty by contrast, he says, and the Prince nodded assent. Apropos Balbo, Bastianini told me about a conversation he had with him in Tripoli. Briefly, Balbo made a profession of love and loyalty towards me...What is behind these declarations? Oaths of loyalty are made to the Chief [Mussolini]—when they are made between comrades they smack of conspiracy, and that I violently repudiate." (August 31, 1937) PREVIOUSLY UNPUBLISHED PHOTO FROM THE HERMANN GÖRING ALBUMS IN THE LIBRARY OF CONGRESS, WASHINGTON, D.C.

Mussolini (left) and Balbo review an air show in 1927. Did Balbo plot to overthrow the Duce? "The majority of these rumors are without substance," answers Claudio Segrè. "Even those that have the most plausibility are far from definitive, as is the case with Balbo's alleged plots against Mussolini in 1931-32. Certainly Balbo did not lack motive. He was an ambitious man, and the more he succeeded the more he aspired to new honors." PHOTO FROM THE U.S. NATIONAL ARCHIVES, COLLEGE PARK, MD which to purchase materials. Balbo's mass flights around the Mediterranean and his transatlantic crossings served as publicity and sales trips to promote industry."

Continues Segrè, "From a purely economic point of view, these policies appear ludicrous. On a long-term basis, Italy could not possibly compete with France, England and Germany. The individual brilliance and intuitions of her best designers and engineers were not enough to sustain an industry. Italy lacked managerial skills, technical facilities and the necessary huge amounts of capital and raw materials. Production figures from World War II illustrate how absurd Italy's pretensions were. In 1941, her peak year, Italy produced 3,503 aircraft; during that year the English and Americans, working far under their maximum capacity, produced nearly six times as many. As their production expanded, by 1944 the Americans produced 96,370 planes annually, and the English 29,220."

Balbo had visited all the major air powers except Japan and realized that his homeland could not expect to compete in the aviation industry. Furthermore, intelligence kept him informed of international developments. "Nevertheless," writes Segrè, "in his mind political and patriotic considerations outweighed economic ones in promoting Italy's aircraft industry. Such a nationalist economic policy, with its emphasis on autarchy and self-sufficiency, was typical of fascism and reflected the protectionist trading policies of the inter-war period. Balbo's one faint hope was that through a restructuring of the armed forces the Aeronautica would enjoy a larger budget and thus would be able to sustain Italy's aircraft industry.

"Like the aircraft industries of the other air powers, Italy's first developed as a crash program during World War I. From 382 aircraft and 606 engines in 1915, the industry boomed to produce 6,523 aircraft and 14,848 engines by 1918. Most of these were of French or English design, although the first Italian designs began to appear during the last years. The expansion of the Balbo era, despite the Aeronautica's limited budget, helped pull the Italian industry out of its postwar slump. In 1926, Italy's aircraft sector consisted of about fourteen aircraft companies and engine manufacturers. The airframe companies employed about 4,300, and the engines, 2,200. In his annual message as minister, Balbo announced that the industry had produced 420 aircraft and 900 engines during the year—a level not

much higher than that of 1915.

"Despite Balbo's efforts to expand the industry, Italy's productive capacities came nowhere near those of its competitors. In 1932/33, Balbo made some estimates of Italy's wartime productive capabilities. Within six months, production could increase to 700 aircraft a month and eventually reach a maximum of 1,000 aircraft a month. Aircraft engine production could increase from 120 units a month to 1,300 or 1,400 units after eighteen months of mobilization. Balbo was proud of his industry's response to a concrete test for summer maneuvers in 1931. Three of the largest companies working alone, Aeronautica d'Italia, Caproni, and Breda, in three months had produced and repaired 600 aircraft and delivered 600 new engines and repaired 550.

"In their productive capacities, however, the other major air powers dwarfed Italy. Germany, although restricted by the Treaty of Versailles, had seventeen aircraft factories, six for engines and three for dirigibles and balloons. In 1932/33, the Italians estimated that their current monthly production was 250 aircraft and 275 motors. After a month of mobilization, it was estimated that Germany could produce 750 aircraft and 860 motors and after a second month could expand to 3,000 aircraft and 4,000 motors. The French and English, too, overwhelmed Italy in scale. In 1932/33, France, the largest manufacturer in the world, boasted forty aircraft companies and ten engine manufacturers with an estimated monthly productive capacity in peacetime of 200 aircraft and 450 engines. England, with thirty aircraft companies and twelve engine manufacturers, produced seventy aircraft a month, but its capabilities were much larger.

"In producing commercial aircraft, estimates ranked Italy (350) with France (373) and Germany (200) in 1932. This was well below Great Britain (470) and the leader, the United States (1,582). The Americans regularly accounted for close to half the world's commercial aircraft.

"A national industry meant independence in raw materials. Balbo worked toward this end. His annual messages to the Chamber of Deputies are full of optimistic indications that Italy could become self-sufficient. Italian researchers experimented with tar as a source of airplane fuel and castor oil as a lubricant. Italy reduced her dependence on Japan for parachute silk and produced her own fabric. New provisions were made to protect her domestic supplies of wood. These efforts failed. The costs of producing substitutes—when that was possible—proved uneconomical. The aircraft companies themselves despite regulations against buying raw materials abroad, did so regularly, because of lower costs.

"Despite these obstacles, Italy took on the appearances of an industrial air power. She exported aircraft, engines, spare parts, and parachutes throughout the world. In 1931 her sales included seven aircraft and forty-four seaplanes for a total of nearly 16 million lire. Her customers ranged from Japan to the Belgian Congo. The largest order that year came from the Soviet Union, which bought sixty-two Isotta Fraschini Asso 750-horsepower engines. In 1933, the Germans considered buying Italian fighters until the German aircraft industry could rebuild and produce its own models.

"In his procurement policies Balbo appears to have been demanding. At first, he looked like an easy mark for the industrialists, for he lacked a technical background. In his first annual message to the Chamber of Deputies in 1927, for instance, he clumsily defended the validity of wood construction airframes against those built of steel and aluminum. 'He is in the hands of the usual meddlers and intriguers, because he knows nothing of the technical aspects and thinks he knows,' snickered Antonio Locatelli, a gold medal winner with D'Annunzio's squadron in World War I, and a deputy. But Balbo relied on highly respected technical experts such as Rodolfo Verduzio, Giulio Constanzi, and Arturo Crocco, and he learned quickly.

"In public, he praised the industry and Italian designers who produced aircraft that won the Schneider Trophy and flew the Atlantic. If Italian designs had not always been highly original in the past, he blamed the government's 'excessive restrictions.' In asking for future bids, Balbo promised that the government would require only a few basic characteristics so that designers would be free to exercise their ingenuity. He also promised—following Verduzio's advice—that in drawing up contracts with the companies, the ministry would not haggle excessively over prices. Such a policy was only an apparent saving; in reality, it led to the use of inferior materials, he claimed.

"Despite these declarations, he earned a reputation for dealing with a firm hand. He described himself as being 'fairly tough with the industrialists and rigorously demanding what industry can and must give me.' At the beginning of his ministry, he took a hard line. On November 19, 1926, he held an important meeting with the major manufacturers, including Caproni, Piaggio and Macchi, in which the two sides sounded each other out. The manufacturers complained about a long list of difficulties with the ministry: slowness of payments, penalties for late consignments, and other bureaucratic problems. In turn, Balbo attacked the industry for its tardiness in making deliveries and fulfilling specifications. He warned them that the ministry would not subsidize ailing companies, and he demanded 'without discussion' that the industry form a consortium for exports. Over the years, he insisted on competitive bidding and the construction of prototypes. Test pilots for the ministry no longer accepted gold watches and other little gifts from the companies for overlooking flaws in the prototypes and failures to meet contract specifications."

Yet soon after Balbo began his tenure at the air ministry, many were gossiping about whether he was playing favorites with manufacturers in the aviation industry. "Some thought he was partial to Fiat because Fiat had helped finance the *Corriere Padano*," explains Segrè. "Others thought he was partial to SIAI because of the SM.55. Yet Balbo's personal integrity was such that it became the subject of an often-repeated anecdote. On a visit to Fiat, the story goes, he was offered a sports car. The president of Fiat, scrupulous about regulations against bribery and favoritism, asked for a symbolic payment of one lira. Balbo drew a two-lira coin from his pocket and presented it to the official. 'I'm sorry, I don't have any change,' the official said. 'That's all right,' Balbo replied. 'Just give me another car!'"

Balbo was a strong-willed CEO. "Although Balbo generally relied on the advice of his technical experts in making procurement decisions, he was quite capable of taking matters into his own hands and riding his own hobbyhorse," writes Segrè. "One example was the affair of the MF 5. In August of 1930, the ministry asked for bids on a design for an Italian seaplane that could become standard equipment on civilian airlines. A Fiat subsidiary, CMASA of Marina di Pisa, designed a twin-engine, all-metal, ten-passenger flying boat developed from the German Dornier 'Wal,' which the company produced under license. Although the designer claimed that the MF 5 met all the contract specifications, Balbo rejected it in 1933. The MF 5 derived from the Dornier models, looked too 'German' for Balbo and he preferred the SM.66, a larger passenger version of his beloved SM.55."

Too, Balbo was capable of errors. "His most colossal—in every sense of the word—procurement blunder," asserts Segrè, "was the DO X. The DO X was the jumbo of its day, a monster flying boat whose twelve engines generated 7,500 horsepower and were theoretically capable of lifting an airframe with a capacity of 150 passengers. Dornier's dream, with this giant, was to supersede dirigibles in transatlantic travel. From its inception in 1926, the project was plagued with engine troubles. Balbo's technical advisers, Costanzi and Verduzio, were divided on the DO X's merits. Nevertheless, Balbo ordered two of the giants in 1931 at a cost of more than 30 million lire—a significant drain on the budget. The DO Xs proved to be white elephants. They were far too large to be used economically on civilian airlines; they were far too unwieldy and unreliable to be used for military purposes. In 1933, the planes were used for training purposes; by 1934, they were no longer flying, and by 1937 they had been scrapped."

Italy developed her first commercial airline during the first seven years of Balbo's reign. Heavily subsidized by the government (up to 50 percent of cost in some years) airline traffic quadrupled during the first few years of operation. "Commercial flights linked all parts of Italy, extended throughout the Mediterranean, and stretched north to Berlin, states Segrè. Balbo encouraged this growth and took pride in it as yet another example of how Italy was marching in the vanguard of 'civilization.' Yet he resented the diversion of funds in his budget away from military purposes, and he doubted whether commercial aviation would ever pay for itself."

Nonetheless, Balbo proudly reported on the growth of commercial aviation. "By 1931," Segrè reports, "the network totaled 16,249 kilometers, four times what it had been in 1926; the numbers of kilometers flown in 1930 was eight times what it had been in 1926, and the number of passengers had increased tenfold. By 1930, with 40,000 passengers carried that year, Italy ranked third in Europe, after Germany and France—and ahead of Great Britain. It was a remarkable achievement.

"In addition to expanding Italy's domestic net, Balbo branched out to establish international and colonial routes. These were problems that required Balbo's personal attention, for together with commercial advantages, the international routes raised issues of national prestige. To highlight the importance of the colonial tie, Balbo personally flew a trial of the Rome-Tripoli line with fourteen passengers on October 2, 1928. He also negotiated the 'line to the Orient' with the British and French. His goal was to share the 'India mail' traffic to Egypt. For prestige reasons, he sought to tie Libya into the network and to secure landing rights in Tunis. 'Thousands and thousands of Italians who live on the African coast in conditions of almost complete isolation from the mother country would now be an hour from Sicily, two hours from Sardegna, and four hours from Rome,' he told the Chamber of Deputies. In March 1928, the French agreed to grant landing rights in Marseilles and Tunis. In return, the Italians gave the French rights to stop in Naples and Castelrosso. Balbo broke a stalemate in negotiations with the British and inaugurated the Genoa-Rome-Alexandria route at the end of March 1929. Balbo also investigated expansion in China and routes to Latin America. The Chinese venture never bore fruit; the Latin American routes were established in 1938-1939, long after Balbo had left the ministry.

"Despite his pride in the development of commercial aviation in Italy, he had serious reservations. 'Civil aviation is not a field that can develop without limit,' he told the Chamber of Deputies in 1929, just after boasting that the industry's statistics had doubled over the previous year. 'Today, all the airlines in the world are in the red' and 'much caution' would be necessary to establish commercial aviation as a public service that would meet the needs of the nation.'"

"In taking this stand, he was undoubtedly following his own convictions, but he may also have been following Mussolini's lead," Segrè postulates. "In a brief memorandum to the minister of finance, Senator Antonio Mosconi, the Duce commented that 'the further progress of commercial airlines (important most of all from a *military* point of view)' required 18 million lire in additional funds for the year 1929/30. However, the airlines had already reached their maximum development, Mussolini concluded."

With an eye to the future, Balbo continued to bemoan commercial aviation's drain on his military budget. "'Since I am convinced that it will be very difficult to utilize civilian aircraft in war, I must focus financial efforts above all on military aviation,' he declared in his 1931 budget message. His skepticism was justified. Although both passenger and freight service had grown by leaps and bounds, the airlines were not carrying anywhere near their capacity, nor were they close to making a profit. As in other European countries," continues Segrè, "the Italian airlines could not have developed without heavy government subsidies. Between 1927 and 1929, these nearly doubled, from 35 million lire annually to 68 million, from 5 to 10 percent of the Aeronautica's annual appropriation. The subsidies in 1928 amounted to about half the cost of operations. In addition, the government took part in the capitalization of the companies and exempted them from customs and other taxes on fuel, lubricants, and necessary imported equipment. In 1931 Balbo commented that the first period of explosive growth was now over and he wanted to establish stable, practical, efficient public service. Passenger and tourist service, he was convinced, would always have only secondary importance for civil aviation. The mails, Balbo felt, would provide the chief rationale for commercial aviation. 'Everything will have to depend on the postal service...whose development already is the pride of all great civilized nations,' he declared.

"To ease the financial straits of the airlines and the drain on the budget, in November of 1933 Balbo drew up a plan to consolidate the competing airlines into a single state-operated airline. At the end of October 1934, the new organization, Ala Littoria, emerged with an operating capital of 18 million lire and seventy-nine aircraft. By that time, Balbo had already been governor-general of Libya for ten months," Segrè concludes.

Budapest, October 10, 1936, for the funeral of Hungarian Minister President Gombös are assembled, left to right: foreground, unknown, German Air Minister Gen. Hermann Göring, Italian Foreign Minister Count Galeazzo Ciano and Austrian President Kurt von Schuschnigg, whom Göring would help overthrow 18 months later when the Nazis took Austria. Having just returned from service with his Regia Aeronautica bombing squadron, Ciano wears his prized Air Force blue uniform. No Balbo fan, in the end he came to agree with his late rival that the German alliance was a disaster for Italy and the Fascist regime, which was toppled because of it. PREVIOUSLY UNPUBLISHED PHOTO FROM THE HERMANN GÖRING ALBUMS IN THE LIBRARY OF CONGRESS, WASHINGTON, D.C.

Balbo (center, smoking cigarette) poses with Regia Aeronautica pilots at an English military air show in 1928. PHOTO FROM THE LIBRARY OF CONGRESS, WASHINGTON, D.C.

German air force men lounge in front of a sign proclaiming their squadron "Luftgeschwader Balbo." Dino Alfieri, the Italian Ambassador to Germany, wrote in 1954: "Balbo did not like the Germans; but this did not prevent him from admiring their methodical ways and their great gifts of organization, nor did it deter him from associating freely with Göring...Balbo was no less popular in Germany than he was in Italy." PREVIOUSLY UNPUBLISHED PHOTO FROM THE HEINRICH HOFFMANN ALBUMS IN THE U.S. NATIONAL ARCHIVES, COLLEGE PARK, MD

Balbo's Hard-Won Independence for the Regia Aeronautica

"Italian journalists distinguished between the British aviator, who was only a 'sportsman,' and the Italian aviator, who 'remains a soldier even when he is an artist.'"
— Claudio Segrè

Balbo was now responsible for a new branch of the military. It was up to him to develop a disciplined air force with a clear sense of mission and a unique set of traditions. Balbo defined his challenge with these words: "The problem in aviation is above all the problem of personnel. It is infinitely more difficult to create a pilot than to build an airplane."

Notes Segrè: "The Aeronautica's spirit and traditions were derived from the individualistic, often anarchic, experiences of World War I. Its relationships with the other armed services were confused and uneasy, and its bureaucracy was not even housed under a single roof. In his seven years as minister, Balbo changed all this. By the time he left, the Aeronautica's blue uniform had captured the imagination of the public and the hearts of young Italians who sought to join its ranks. The men who wore the uniform knew that they belonged to a legitimate service with traditions, regulations, and a mission. Naturally, Balbo did not always succeed. For example, his struggle with the other services left bitterness, confusion, and uncertainty about the Aeronautica's mission—but this was not unique to Italy.

"Recruitment for the Aeronautica was a difficult task at first. Without the prestige and traditions of the army and navy, the Aeronautica had a hard time attracting young men inclined to a military career. To fill the ranks, many pilots—and other personnel as well—came from the other services...the Aeronautica held no fewer than six special competitions for officers and NCOs needed to fill the ranks. These included 200 sergeants for ground crews, 400 for flight crews, and 100 officers for reserves. Other competitions sought officers from the army and navy to fill both active duty and reserve positions. These last would be eliminated as soon as the service's immediate needs were met, Balbo promised. For the sake of morale, an air force career had to begin at the bottom and not at the top, he declared.

"Another personnel problem to which for obvious reasons he did not refer, was the conflict between cliques and the inter-service rivalry within the Aeronautica. An anonymous 'Commander Nemo' informed him regularly of the feuds between former navy and former army men. Balbo tried to attract pilots from World War I to the Aeronautica's reserves. With his instinct for publicity, he thought of new ways to promote the Aeronautica and flying, both civilian and military. The Office of Civil Aviation, the ministry's press office and the Aero Club d'Italia all dispensed information. Aerial cruises, displays and pageantry, air races, and flying tours of Italy generated interest in aviation and attracted recruits. By 1932, Balbo claimed that the Aeronautica had so many aspirants to become pilots that the service could afford to reject 80 percent of them on the basis of a physical examination."

"Thanks to these efforts," Segrè adds, "the Aeronautica grew in size and began to take on the composition of a professional fighting force. The 1925 Bonzani regulations provided for 2,340 officers; Balbo's regulations of 1931 provided for 3,060, an increase of about a third. Within the flying branch during the years 1925 and 1931, there was also a notable increase in the numbers of officers from captain to general and in the non-commissioned officers. The numbers of subalterns and enlisted men diminished. This reflected the large increase in professional men in the ranks—those who were committed to a career in the Aeronautica or who had, at least, voluntarily signed up for a long-term period of service. By 1930, Italy could claim 3,000 pilots, three for every one of her available military aircraft—without counting those in the reserves, Balbo claimed proudly. This was almost quadruple the cadre provided for in 1926.

"The organization also began to show increased specialization. For example, the 1931 regulations created a service section within the flying branch. This was to employ personnel who, for various reasons, could no longer fly but could still serve usefully on the ground...Nevertheless, if numbers of support personnel for every pilot are an indication of an air force's sophistication, Italy lagged well behind the other powers. In 1927 Balbo reported that Italy had the lowest ratio of personnel per plane and the lowest ratio of nonflying to flying personnel of any of the major air powers. For every aircraft in service, England had fifty-three support persons, France twenty-nine, Germany thirty-four. Italy had only seventeen.

"While the Aeronautica's numbers increased steadily, Balbo lobbied for an even larger service. For example, in the 1931 regulations, the Aeronautica was allowed 3,060 officers, with 1,750 of them assigned to the flying branch. In practice, when parliament voted appropriations, it authorized personnel increases on a year-to-year basis. For 1931/32, parliament authorized 2,160 officers, 4,000 NCOs, and 18,000 enlisted men. The Aeronautica's real strength fell short even of that. As of January 1, 1932, there were 1,700 officers (1,100 of them in the flying branch), 3,100 NCOs and 16,000 enlisted men. Was the Aeronautica short-handed? Probably not. The staff that Balbo sought had little to do with the Aeronautica's real need and capacities at the moment. He wanted to create an opening for future development and to show the Aeronautica's emergence as a power under his direction.

"Critics sniped that those who aspired to join the Aeronautica came for reasons other than simple love of flying. They wanted to take advantage of faster promotions and special medals and honors for those who took part in activities such as the aerial cruises. While this may have been true initially, by the early 1930s the ranks had filled and the early careers and fast promotions had disappeared. Sixty percent of the officers, Balbo declared in 1932, would complete their careers as captains. The other 40 percent, who reached the higher ranks, had to meet stiff standards both of technical competence as pilots and of leadership ability. As Balbo pointed out, the age limit for the highest rank, *generale di squadra aerea* [general of air squadron], was 55; the average age for the few generals in the next two ranks below was 48 and 46, respectively.

"Filling the ranks, of course, was not enough; Balbo also sought to imbue his men with pride in their organization and with ideals worth fighting for. As the newest of the services, created under fascism, the Aeronautica gained a reputation for being the most fascist of the armed forces," states Segrè. "Balbo had molded a fascist air force while Gazzara had created an anti-fascist army, sneered Farinacci. He was wrong. One of Balbo's great achievements was that, under his direction, the Aeronautica came to be accepted as a legitimate armed service on a par with the army and the navy."

Balbo fostered the concept of the professional soldier and believed that the military had no business mixing in politics, except as private citizens. Segrè explains the two ways Balbo made his stand clear: "First, he refused to allow politics to affect promotions. He personally decided on those whom he felt worthy of party membership and restricted the number severely. He urged the party secretary [Achille Starace] to ignore any requests that did not come directly from him. He protested when a local party secretary publicly distributed party cards to officers on active duty.

"Second, Balbo made his attitudes toward politics and his ideas about the proper conduct for an officer explicit in a circular of December 6, 1927. Under the heading 'Moral and Political Education of Airmen,' he urged his officers to speak out in favor of fascism. In doing so, he referred to no specific organization and no particular personality. He equated fascism quite simply with national pride...

"Balbo's code of behavior for his officers was thoroughly conventional. He expected them to behave like gentlemen...Irregular relationships—illegal marriages or mistresses—would not be tolerated, he warned...Gossips and critics were admonished to control their tongues, for, Balbo noted, foreign air attachés were not only up on the latest developments in the Aeronautica, but also knew all the gossip. Finally, off duty and away from their bases, officers might participate in social life as much as they liked, but air bases were for training, not for aerial joy rides, dancing, teas and tennis with girl friends and wives...

"He gained a reputation for punishing infractions severely, and he turned down appeals...

"One of Balbo's major battles in the Aeronautica was with the aces and *prime donne*. With them he was even more demanding and inflexible than with the rank and file. He played a major role in ruining the careers of De Pinedo and Nobile. Lesser personalities such as Mario De Bernardi and Arturo Ferrarin preferred not to tangle with him. Even Stefano Cagna, his personal pilot for many years, a veteran of all of Balbo's major aerial cruises, got a cold shoulder when he violated Balbo's sense of duty. In April 1940, on the eve of the war, Cagna had resigned from the Aeronautica to take a position in civil aviation. 'Your departure, even if it left me with a bad impression, certainly has not changed my feelings with regard to you,' Balbo reassured him. Nevertheless, 'I really cannot wish you anything in your new activity except that very soon you will give it up for an important command or a delicate military mission where a young general can best serve the service and the Fatherland.'

"Balbo's great goal, he declared in his annual message to the Chamber of Deputies in 1929, was to imbue Italian aviation with 'a military spirit, which...would take into account the wholesome individualism of every flyer.' Nevertheless, each pilot must develop a sense of duty that would go beyond mere individual achievements to include a feeling of belonging to a larger organization. On March 28, 1933, the tenth anniversary of the founding of the Aeronautica, and six and a half years after Balbo became head of the Aeronautica, he declared that he had 'definitely eradicated the excessive spirit of individualism that diminished the military character of the service'; he had created a healthy and high esprit de corps, and he had restored discipline."

And what of technical merit? Asserts Segrè, "To judge by their world's records, their victories in air races such as the Schneider Cup, their aerobatic teams that performed throughout Europe and the United States, Balbo's disciplined Italian pilots ranked among the best in the world. Critics, however,...[claimed]...too much of the Aeronautica's training was devoted to special events...not enough to preparing the rank and file.

"Balbo frequently declared that he was committed to...building an Aeronautica in which every man would be extraordinary. He did work hard to overhaul the chaotic system of training. Until 1929 seven civilian aviation schools (all private enterprises) used about thirty different types of machines to carry out a three-stage training program. In that year Balbo appointed a military commission that standardized both the program and the machines and reduced the training costs. Flying in these schools in 1927 totaled 30,000 hours, about half the total hours of military pilots for that year, and more than five hundred students successfully completed the civilian courses in 1929.

"Balbo also introduced several specialty schools. The Scuola di Alta Velocita [School of High Velocity] at Desenzano for research and development at high speeds began operations in April 1928, and the Scuola di Navigazione Aerea di Alto Mare [School of Navigation] at Orbetello began operations on January 1, 1930, as a center for training crews for long-range oceanic cruises. At Roma-Ciampino, he also developed a center to test and train pilots in Mecozzi's assault tactics; at Udine-Campoformido he supported a unit that specialized in aerobatics; and at Montecelio he favored a center for research in high-altitude flying." Continues Segrè, "The fates of Desenzano and Orbetello, in particular, support the argument that Balbo had created these programs for very limited purposes. Desenzano's mission was really to pursue the Schneider Cup with greater method; Orbetello's to train crews for the Atlantic cruises. Once Balbo left the Aeronautica, the programs faded away—Desenzano as early as 1936.

"Meanwhile, those who were not involved in these special projects flew relatively little, as the statistics illustrate. To be sure, flying time in the Aeronautica increased more than two and a half times, from 50,400 hours in 1926 to 139,400 in 1931. However, so did the number of aircraft and the number of pilots. The Aeronautica's flying time in 1931 was only about half that of the estimates for the French Air Force (250,000-400,000 hours) and the RAF (325,000 hours) and about a third of the total for the American army and navy (670,000 hours). The Aeronautica's flying time per aircraft was also relatively limited. In 1930, for example, fighters averaged 150 hours, bombers 70 hours, land reconnaissance 190 hours, and sea reconnaissance 170. Accidents were relatively frequent. In 1927, for example, there were 581 accidents, with 58 dead, 19 seriously injured, and 260 aircraft destroyed. In 1931, 25 officers and 38 NCOs had to leave the service because of accidents. Conscious of this problem, Balbo eagerly pointed out signs of improvement. In 1933, for the period up to May 1, there had been only 8 flying fatalities, compared to 30 the previous year with the same number of flying hours, he proclaimed.

"With his taste for display, Balbo emphasized aerial shows such as the two Wing Days (Giornata dell'Ala) held on June 8, 1930 and May 27, 1932. These exhibitions were consciously patterned after the RAF displays at Hendon that were held annually from 1920 to 1938. Like their Hendon counterparts, Wing Days were nominally staged to raise money for air force charities—in the Italian case, an orphanage under the protection of the Madonna di Loreto, the patron saint of aviators. To prove that the Wing Days were not a 'slavish' foreign imitation, Italian journalists distinguished between the British aviator, who was only a 'sportsman,' and the Italian aviator, who 'remains a soldier even when he is an artist.'

"The programs were elaborately choreographed.

Air Marshal Balbo (right) greets German visitors to Rome in 1933. PREVIOUSLY UNPUBLISHED PHOTO FROM THE HEINRICH HOFFMANN ALBUMS IN THE U.S. NATIONAL ARCHIVES, COLLEGE PARK, MD

Nazi fans surround Air Marshal Italo Balbo (center) during the visit of Reich Propaganda Minister Dr. Joseph Goebbels to Italy in 1933. PREVIOUSLY UNPUBLISHED PHOTO FROM THE HEINRICH HOFFMANN ALBUMS IN THE U.S. NATIONAL ARCHIVES, COLLEGE PARK, MD

April 10, 1933: German Luftwaffe Commander-in-Chief Hermann Göring jokes with Air Marshal Italo Balbo (left) during a visit to Rome. PREVIOUSLY UNPUBLISHED PHOTO FROM THE HERMANN GÖRING ALBUMS IN THE LIBRARY OF CONGRESS, WASHINGTON, D.C.

Spectacular aerobatics and elaborate formations, mock attacks on an 'Arab village' and a mass parachute jump comprised the program of the first Wing Day. For the grand finale, 200 planes attacked an 'enemy' airport and chased each other around in vivid dogfights. The 'curtain' came down when a squadron of fighters laid down a smoke screen. 'It was a triumph for Balbo,' De Bono noted in his diary...The show was 'brilliantly conceived and carried out, and we were treated to a show rivaling that of the Royal Air Force Pageant at Hendon,' wrote a foreign guest attending Balbo's 1932 Congress of Trans-Oceanic Aviators. 'I doubt if any pilots of any other nation could have surpassed them,' he concluded.''

Balbo also organized large-scale aerial maneuvers to test Douhet's ideas on the effectiveness of massive aerial attacks. "Two aerial divisions of seventy squadrons each, totaling 860 aircraft, participated in the maneuvers, which lasted from August 26 to September 3 [1931]," writes Segrè. "For three days, each side carried out day—and sometimes night—bombings against major Italian cities...For the finale, 300 planes carried out day and night attacks on Milan.

"Officially, Douhet triumphed. A nation that experienced such an aerial invasion surrendered unconditionally, according to the official communiqué. However, Badoglio, then chief of the supreme general staff, still denied the value of air power, and bitterly criticized the official communiqué. More significantly, the conclusions of the experts and the official results were never made known. Most important, Balbo never repeated such maneuvers. The following year, in August and September, he cooperated with the army in maneuvers, and in October the Aeronautica carried out an experimental bombing of Rome.

"Wing Days and aerial maneuvers were ways of showing off the Aeronautica's prowess before a domestic audience. For the international stage, the major display was for the Schneider Cup. With the famous American competitions, the Thompson, Bendix, Pulitzer and Gordon Bennett, the Schneider ranked as one of the great air racing classics of the pre-World War II period. The French steel and munitions baron Jacques Schneider (1878-1928) first offered the cup in 1912. His goal was to stimulate the development of flying boats, and he dreamed of linking the world by means of flying fleets that did not require expensive airfields.

"By the time Balbo first became involved, the Schneider had evolved into something quite different from what its founder had intended. In the Cup trials between 1926 and 1931, the entries were no longer flying boats, but racing float planes, more advanced than their land-based counterparts. Like racing cars, the Schneider entries demanded enormous amounts of money and effort to develop. The competition, the critics complained, had degenerated into a madcap struggle for speed supremacy—and national prestige. The planes were built exclusively for racing.

"Balbo took office a week before Italy's greatest triumph in the series, the 1926 competition held at Hampton Roads, Virginia, on November 13. The Italians, with three Macchi M.39s, captured both first and third places. Mario de Bernardi piloted the winning entry at an average of 396.689 km/h. In less than nine months, the Italians had produced a design that set the standard for future seaplanes racers—slim fuselage, low-set monoplane wing, liquid-cooled, in-line engine. Four days after the Schneider competition, De Bernardi set a world speed record of 416.618 km/h."

"For the next five years, Balbo pursued the Schneider Cup fruitlessly. The 1927 competition in Venice was particularly humiliating for Italy, and for Balbo. A quarter of a million spectators jammed the length of the fashionable Lido. Of the three M.52s prepared for the race on September 26, not one completed the course. Mechanical failures plagued each one. The British, the only other competitors, had only to complete the course to claim victory. As a consolation that year, on November 4 De Bernardi set another speed record of 479.290 km/h, faster than the winning Schneider time.

"The failure was particularly bitter because on paper the Italians should have won. They had made some excellent test runs, in some cases easily surpassing the eventual winning time. On the other hand, both Italians and foreign observers agreed that the Italians, perhaps overconfident from their startling success the year before, had not prepared seriously and methodically enough for the race. The aircraft companies were contacted too late about building a new engine. Balbo should have agreed to a two-week postponement of the race, as the Americans requested. The Italians would then have had time to test their engines, which proved so unreliable. Even Balbo admitted to Mussolini that the engines had not been sufficiently tried. Balbo's informants hinted that rivalries among the pilots also contrib-

Balbo proudly viewed construction of the air ministry building, an imposing structure topped with pilot wings set in concrete, as a sign of the Aeronautica's bureaucratic and legal independence from the army and navy. "When the Aeronautica was founded," relates Claudio Segrè, "the ministry as scattered in 12 offices throughout the city. Communication between the offices required mountains of paper, squads of messengers, and weeks of time, claimed Balbo. Security was a problem. Finally, and perhaps most important, the physical separation of the offices worked against the creation of a unified spirit within the Service...Balbo's ideas for the building came from his visits to the United States, where he had carefully studied such facilities. The exterior—spare, bare and sober—reflected perfectly the interior rule of life, he claimed." PREVIOUSLY UNPUBLISHED PHOTO FROM THE HERMANN GÖRING ALBUMS IN THE LIBRARY OF CONGRESS, WASHINGTON, D.C.

The courtyard of the air ministry building echoes the simplicity of the building's interior. "Balbo," writes Segrè, "planned bright, open offices where glass replaced walls; he included pneumatic mail service, internal telephones, modern elevators. Everything was adapted to extreme speed and to the silent movement of a complex of 1,200 employees. Visitors remarked on the sparseness...of the furnishings—no armchairs, no rugs, no curtains. Everyone sat on simple wooden chairs." PREVIOUSLY UNPUBLISHED PHOTO FROM THE HERMANN GÖRING ALBUMS IN THE LIBRARY OF CONGRESS, WASHINGTON, D.C.

Fascist Eagle

Located in Rome's Castro Pretorio section, the air ministry building was inaugurated in 1931 as part of celebrations commemorating the March on Rome. Pictured is the cornerstone of the building. PREVIOUSLY UNPUBLISHED PHOTO FROM THE HERMANN GÖRING ALBUMS IN THE LIBRARY OF CONGRESS, WASHINGTON, D.C.

uted to the poor preparation."

"Undaunted," Segrè continues, "Balbo made two decisions to improve Italy's chances in future competitions. First, in agreement with the English, the race was scheduled for every other year. Second, he established the research and testing center at Desenzano. Matters did not improve at the 1929 competition held September 7 at Calshot on England's south coast near Southampton. Four companies, Fiat, Macchi, SIAI and Piaggio, prepared four different models for entry into the race. Fires, crashes and other disasters destroyed nearly all of them. Dal Molin claimed a respectable second for Italy in an old Macchi M.52R, a slightly modified version of the model that had been victorious in 1926. It was a good showing, considering that his engine produced 900 horsepower less than the winner.

"The British needed only one more victory to claim the trophy permanently. So expensive and dangerous had the race become that governments balked at sponsoring it. The 1926 victory had cost the Italians 3,860,000 lire, more than five times that of the previous year; by 1929, the costs had risen to 14,650,000 lire. The aircraft companies bid grudgingly for the Schneider contract and only on the condition that the government provide comfortable subsidies. In parliament, deputies protested that the Schneider cost too much and produced no practical results, Balbo defended the value of the Schneider both as a means of technical progress and as a training exercise. British and French public statements about disinterest were merely posturing, he declared. If they thought they had a chance to win it,

they would once again show interest, he claimed. With the French, he asked for a postponement of the race to allow time for more training and development, but the British declined. Macchi and Fiat teamed up once again to produce the MC.72. A Fiat AS 6 engine—actually two coupled AS 5 engines—powered the aircraft; the development took longer than expected, and after a fatal crash the Italians withdrew. On September 12, a Supermarine S.6B completed the course at Calshot at an average speed of 547.188 km/h, and the British claimed the Schneider Trophy permanently.

"How much the Aeronautica benefited from the Schneider races and the subsequent speed development at Desenzano is still a subject of considerable debate. The research and development for the racing engines continued after the Schneider competition ended. Agello continued to set records with the MC.72. On October 23, 1934, at Desenzano, he piloted a 3,300 horsepower aircraft to a record of 709.202 km/h. (440.681 mph). That speed, of course, has long since been surpassed, but the record still stands for aircraft of that type. Yet the MC.72 had no real influence on standard Italian fighter design. Some claim that the World War II Macchi 202 and 205 were offspring; others argue that the only factor in common is the aircraft company name. Moreover, in 1933, for reasons that are still unclear, the Italian air ministry decided to give up on the development of in-line liquid-cooled engines in favor of air-cooled radial engines. Thus, all the development that went into the Schneider engines was abandoned. The English, in the meantime, based on experience with their Schneider engines, developed the Rolls Royce Merlin that powered their best World War II Spitfire and Hurricane fighters and even the American Mustang. The Italians in 1940 had to rely on German liquid-cooled engines built under license."

"For these reasons, Balbo's critics have dismissed his support of the Schneider races as wasted effort," notes Segrè. "This hardly seems fair. Balbo gave Italian aviation an opportunity. By participating in the Schneider competition, Italy shared in the wealth of new technical developments in designs, fuels, engines, cooling systems, superchargers, and flying techniques. The Schneider racers were so advanced technically that it took four or five years for the rest of the aeronautical world to catch up. If his successors missed the chance, this was hardly Balbo's fault. The Schneider was important in another way: at a time when there was little money for aviation, the races kept public attention focused on flying. Such benefits may be intangible, yet in evaluating Balbo's participation in the Schneider races they cannot be ignored.

"In addition to winning races and gaining public support, Balbo, like the other air ministers of the inter-war period—whether Hermann Göring in Germany or Pierre Cot in France—was concerned with establishing an independent Aeronautica equal in every respect to the army and the navy. Training, esprit, and air shows were not enough. The Aeronautica had to have bureaucratic and legal independence...

"One of his first great innovations was the American-style work schedule—a great shock to government employees accustomed to lunch at home and perhaps a little nap before resuming their office work. Balbo allowed only forty minutes for lunch; at noon—early by Roman standards—everyone ate in the [new air ministry] building's dining hall at the same time. 'Long rows of black marble tables, desk-high, chromium-trimmed (a glorified Child's restaurant),' according to the American racing pilot Major Al Williams, who visited it in 1936. He, like nearly every other visitor, was astonished at another detail. 'There were no chairs in the room—these officers were eating their luncheon standing.' His host explained proudly, 'We have chairs, of course—the space for them—but no time for them.'

"Balbo defended his work schedule zealously. Among its other advantages, he claimed, was that it promoted a better family life. Employees who came to work at eight or eight-thirty could be home with their families at three-thirty or four o'clock in the afternoon. From time to time, he wandered about the ministry to see that employees were observing the schedule. To his undersecretary, who had sent a memorandum that the hours must be respected, Balbo commented tartly, 'The warning is excellent, but one hundred percent useless...if you personally set a bad example, arriving at the office not at eight but after ten. Get up early and at eight make the rounds of the offices...That's the way to command...This is not just an order, but also a friendly bit of advice.'...

"Balbo not only regulated the hours and the environment in which the ministry employees ate lunch, he also tried to regulate *how* they ate. Each employee received a little handbook on good table manners. The reader was carefully instructed on the use of forks and knives...The reader also learned of the correct posture while eating on his feet and was ordered to stand ten centimeters from the table...

"On the surface, Balbo's concern with these details appears to be one more manifestation of the tyrannical side of his nature. Undoubtedly there is some truth in this. Yet it is also important to keep the context in mind. Balbo was struggling to give the Aeronautica legitimacy and respect, to mold a first generation of officers and civilian employees who looked and behaved according to the highest standards of European military tradition and civil service," concludes Segrè.

The new air ministry building was an important symbol of the Aeronautica's independence. Nonetheless, as Segrè goes on to explain, "The problem of the Aeronautica's relationship to the other services remained. According to the statute of 1925, the Aeronautica was divided into four sections: the 'aerial army' proper, consisting of seventy-eight squadrons; army aviation, fifty-seven squadrons; naval aviation, thirty-five squadrons; and colonial aviation, twelve squadrons. The statute was obviously a compromise. To mitigate their jealousies, the senior services retained substantial air forces of their own. At the same time, the Aeronautica had sufficient numbers of its own to create an independent aerial force. Balbo was not satisfied. The Aeronautica was not recognized as an independent force capable of fighting its own battles, he insisted. As soon as he came to the ministry, he laid claim to the air forces assigned to the navy and the army."

Segrè notes that, in this context, Balbo was a model disciple of Douhet. "'Auxiliary aviation' (those

September 29, 1937: Italian Army Field Marshal and Chief of Staff Pietro Badoglio (left) shares a laugh with German Defense Minister and Army Field Marshal Werner von Blomberg while viewing the giant military parade held in Berlin to honor the Duce during his visit to the Third Reich. Badoglio viewed air power as an auxiliary weapon to both the army and navy and persistently criticized Balbo's position that the Regia Aeronautica should be developed as an independent striking force. PREVIOUSLY UNPUBLISHED PHOTO FROM THE HERMANN GÖRING ALBUMS IN THE LIBRARY OF CONGRESS, WASHINGTON, D.C.

Balbo's Hard-Won Independence

air forces assigned to the other services) was 'useless...harmful...superfluous,' Douhet argued in a memorandum to Balbo.

"Both theory and experience, Balbo told parliament, had established the organic unity of aerial defense. The air was a theater independent of the other theaters of operation; it must be entrusted exclusively to the 'aerial army, in which all the available offensive and defensive forces are united'; he was also quite certain that 'the decisive action in future conflicts will be entrusted to the aerial army.' The Aeronautica's unity of command and action must not be weakened by dividing up its forces and its missions.

"In challenging the army and the navy for their air forces, Balbo was breaking down a door that was already half open. Neither of the senior services had much faith in the role of aviation. So long as their budgets were not cut, they did not oppose Balbo vigorously. First the navy, in a meeting of January 27, 1928, gave in on the issue of the auxiliary forces. The assistant chief of staff for the navy, Romeo Bernotti, engaged in a spirited discussion with Balbo. The relationship of the Aeronautica and naval aviation, he argued, should not be decided on the basis of abstract principles such as Balbo proposed, but according to the concrete military problems that Italy might face. His superior, Ernesto Burzaggli, the naval chief of staff, interrupted him: 'That's enough. We give in.' The army's turn came in April, and once again there was no real opposition. The army assumed that airplanes would play much the same role that they had in World War I—useful mostly as artillery spotters, reconnaissance, and couriers. The navy agreed to cut their aerial forces from thirty-five squadrons to eighteen, the army from fifty-seven to forty-six squadrons. The army also accepted Balbo's demand that their airplanes be used only for reconnaissance. The negotiations with the army dragged on for at least two years, however, and relations between the two services deteriorated.

"Balbo, in the meantime, aspired to draw up a statute to reflect the Aeronautica's new status. The army found an ally in the finance ministry, which resented Balbo's cavalier way of dealing with the state's accounting methods. Balbo's proposal was blocked when he brought it before the Council of Ministers in June 1930. Mussolini, who did not want to show favoritism, preferred to have the service chiefs resolve the matter among themselves. Balbo, however, appealed directly to him in a letter of June 16, 1930. 'Today, even after so many proofs of competence and sacrifice before you and Italy, I feel clearly that the independence and maturity of the Royal Air Force is not finding among all the ministers its proper recognition. Give me a chance to defend these ideas in your presence,' he pleaded. Balbo succeeded, and in January 1931, his new set of statutes was approved by the parliament. They did not differ radically from those of 1925 except that the forces assigned to the army and the navy were reduced.

"Balbo won another struggle with the navy—the battle over aircraft carriers. 'You want aircraft carriers, but I shall not let you build them,' he told Admiral Bernotti. Carriers were superfluous for Italy, he argued—and he had many supporters. Italy itself—the peninsula, Sicily and Sardinia—formed a natural carrier, a much cheaper and more secure one than a vessel, Balbo argued. From land bases, the Aeronautica's aircraft had sufficient range to strike all vital points in the Mediterranean. His opposition to building battleships, however, failed. Despite his contention that air power was cheaper and that a battle fleet was too vulnerable in a narrow sea like the Mediterranean, the navy prevailed.

"In his struggle with the other services to assert the independence of the Aeronautica, Balbo won. So far as the nation's defense was concerned, however, his was a Pyrrhic victory. In practice, each service prepared for its own war, and coordination among the branches was ignored. The Aeronautica never developed a clear sense of its role. The effects became evident in 1940 when the Italians failed in their attacks on the British Fleet in the Mediterranean and in their bombings of English cities."

Believes Segrè, "The fault certainly did not lie only with Balbo. The responsibility for coordinating the three services lay with Mussolini. He might easily have created a defense ministry or a general chief of staff with powers over all three services. Balbo made such proposals in 1933 and Mussolini repeatedly turned them down. Such an office, particularly with Balbo at the head of it, as he proposed, posed too great a political threat to the dictator. Italy paid dearly for this decision in 1940. Balbo, too, perhaps paid dearly for his battle with the other services," concludes Segrè. "With better coordination, the anti-aircraft batteries might have been aware of who was approaching the airfield at Tobruk on June 28, 1940." As it happened, Balbo's plane was shot down and he was killed.

From Air Marshal to World Class Aviator

"Balbo the radical republican had disappeared."
—Claudio Segrè

By the time of his death on June 28, 1940, Italian Air Marshal Italo Balbo's fame rested on three pillars. The first was his leadership of the fascist militia during the March on Rome in 1922. The second was his creation of the Regia Aeronautica, and the third his tour of duty as the governor general of the Italian colony of Libya.

The highly publicized mass-formation aerial cruises that Balbo led or participated in between 1928 and 1933 were an important component of his tenure as air minister. These awe-inspiring cruises gained Balbo international fame and, in Claudio Segrè's words, "a lasting reputation as one of aviation's great pioneers."

By 1926 the accomplishments of aviators such as Francesco De Pinedo, Arturo Ferrarin, and Mario De Bernardi, had established Italy's reputation in the aviation world. While Balbo "welcomed the publicity they provided for the development of flying in general and for the Aeronautica in particular," notes Segrè, "he opposed the mentality of the *prima donna* and the *diva*, which he claimed went with such record flights...It was very difficult to force the great champions to submit to military discipline, he declared in 1929. There were also personal considerations. Some of the *dive*, such as the glamorous Francesco De Pinedo, aspired to be at least Balbo's equal. Others, like Umberto Nobile, with his dedication to airships rather than airplanes, were, in Balbo's view, leading the Aeronautica down a blind alley."

Partly to offset this *prima donna* mentality and the corresponding image of "only a few good men" in the Regia Aeronautica, Balbo conceived the plan for mass formation flights. "The flights, thanks to the fascist propaganda machine, enjoyed enormous publicity," claims Segrè in *Italo Balbo: A Fascist Life*. "Heroism was not abolished, but instead of being individual, it became collective. He did the extraordinary with the aim of transforming it into the ordinary. The ultimate goal of his transatlantic flights was to make such crossings routine.

"Balbo's notion of mass flights was certainly not original with him. Italian aviation had a well-estab- lished tradition along these lines. Douhet had first suggested the idea of great aerial fleets, and during the waning days of World War I, at the Battle of Vittorio Veneto, the Italians experimented with such formations. Balbo was also deeply indebted to De Pinedo, who was internationally recognized as one of the great pioneers of long-distance flight...

"For his aerial cruises, Balbo followed De Pinedo's example with regard to flying boats...He depended heavily on De Pinedo's skills as an organizer and as a pilot, for he was not himself an exceptional pilot. During a flying career that lasted about fourteen years, Balbo totaled about 3,000 flying hours, a good but not an extraordinary total. Unlike the best airmen, he did not handle seaplanes as well as land planes. Because he knew his limitations, for years he kept Stefano Cagna, a truly outstanding pilot, as his flying aide. At first, in organizing the aerial cruises, Balbo had the good sense to rely on more experienced and talented pilots. De Pinedo provided the leadership for the two Mediterranean cruises. For the first Atlantic expedition in 1931 to Brazil, Balbo called on Umberto Maddalena, who, like Cagna, was personally close to Balbo and one of the Aeronautica's most skilled pilots. By 1933, for the last of the four major aerial cruises, Balbo felt experienced and self-confident enough to take charge himself.

"Of these four major aerial cruises, the first was by far the largest in terms of men and equipment. Sixty-one seaplanes transported a party of nearly two hundred to ports of the Western Mediterranean from May 26 to June 2, 1928. Beginning from Orbetello, the huge expedition made six stops: Elmas (Sardegna), Pollensa (Balearic Islands), Los Alcazares and Puerto Alfaques (Spain), Berre (France), and Orbetello. The route was chosen according to specific criteria. The distance between each pair of ports was no more than about five hundred kilometers or three to four hours of flying time. Each stop offered a bay large enough to accommodate the entire formation, provide good anchorage and was easy to supply. The bulk of the aircraft were fifty-one SIAI reconnaissance planes and light bombers with 500-horsepower engines. The remaining ten aircraft consisted of SM.55s like the one De Pinedo used in his long-distance flights, and one

In 1928 Balbo's armada of Savoia Marchetti SM.55Xs soared over the Italian Alps in a breathtaking display that captured the imagination of the world. PHOTO FROM THE LIBRARY OF CONGRESS, WASHINGTON, D.C.

This Savoia Marchetti SM.55X flying boat sports Italian national tail markings and a single fasces emblem on each of its two wooden bows. PHOTO FROM THE U.S. NATIONAL ARCHIVES, COLLEGE PARK, MD

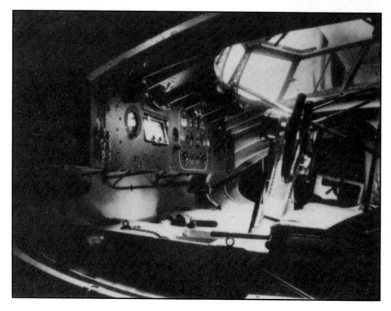

A view of the Savoia Marchetti SM.55X cockpit and instrument panel. PHOTO FROM THE CAPRONI MUSEUM ARCHIVE, ROME, ITALY

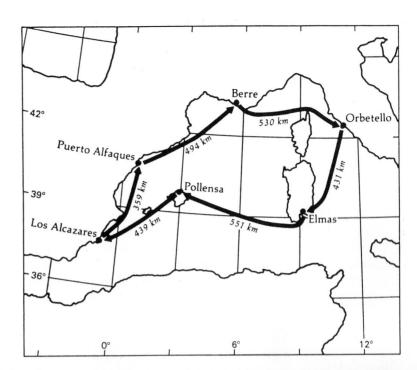

Balbo's first mass formation aerial cruise was a tour of the Western Mediterranean in 1928. Balbo, says Claudio Segrè, "envisioned formation flying as a form of close-order drill that taught the value of command, of discipline, of performing as a group. He denied that he was creating an elite. With proper training and leadership, even an average pilot could participate in these expeditions, Balbo claimed. He also stressed the cultural benefits of the cruises. His men would come in contact with new peoples and new customs." ADAPTED FROM G.B. GUERRI'S *ITALO BALBO*

Cant.22. These carried the observers: dignitaries, high-ranking officers, journalists and foreign military attachés, including those from France, Spain, England and the United States."

"The scale of the formation was unprecedented," writes Segrè. "Prior to this...such flights had been carried out with no more than eight aircraft. When the full expedition lined up, wing tip to wing tip, the row of aircraft stretched for four kilometers. Such a large formation was vulnerable to the open sea, and critics charged that more than five aircraft would be lost on each leg. Nevertheless, with Mussolini's blessing...Balbo went ahead.

"Except for a storm which led to some minor collisions while the fleet was anchored at Los Alcazares, the operation went smoothly. As the expedition progressed, the pilots became increasingly skilled and confident in their formation work, and the expedition made a great show. In the air they formed four arrowheads around a diamond. So tight was the formation that the planes looked suspended from invisible threads, wrote one journalist; so huge was the formation that in flight the nearest aircraft looked like 'eagles' and the most distant like 'flies.' Even more spectacular were the takeoffs and landings. At Orbetello, the expedition took off squadron by squadron. Nine by nine, as if dancing a quadrille, each squadron taxied into the wind; then, as one, they gathered speed, reached the 'step,' broke from the water's surface, and lifted off, leaving nine parallel churning white furrows—the wakes—behind them.

By the time the expedition reached Puerto Alfaques, the pilots were skilled enough to take off en masse, and the town marveled at the spectacle of all sixty-one aircraft lifting off simultaneously. Their tight formation over Marseilles brought cheers from the spectators on the ground.

"Balbo's role during the Western Mediterranean cruise was minor. He flew about as he pleased, and while the expedition was anchored at Los Alcazares, he lunched in Madrid with the king of Spain. The real leader of the expedition was De Pinedo. Balbo generously acknowledged this in a final press conference...At his own suggestion, as a reward for his role in the expedition, Balbo enjoyed a meteoric promotion. First, Mussolini promoted Balbo to the rank of reserve general in the air force and then called him to active duty. From a militia general, Mussolini had magically transformed him into a real general...De Pinedo, too, received promotions in rank and position, as well as the title of marquis."

Continues Segrè, "Less than a month after his return...Balbo led a parody of an aerial cruise. The trip came to be known euphemistically as the Cruise of the European Capitals...The cruise's main destination was London, to attend the RAF annual air display at nearby Hendon. The expedition violated all Balbo's carefully enunciated principles about earlier cruises. The twenty-four pilots were all senior men with long experience, not ordinary pilots from regular units; the dozen planes were not seaplanes, but twelve land planes—six A.120s and six R.22s; the expedition did not train together for formation flying; Balbo apparently gave no thought to logistics and ground support. He sent one of his aides ahead by train to determine the location of the London airport. The expedition left June 28 for the 1,600 km flight to London via Paris. Only half the aircraft arrived that day. Four landed in France, two in Belgium and one in the Netherlands. The remaining six straggled in at various intervals, 'like sheep.' How so many experienced pilots became so lost, Balbo never explained...[In England] The air minister, Sir Samuel Hoare, and the chief of the air staff, Lord Hugh Trenchard, hosted Balbo. He toured major aircraft factories...

"The cruise next flew to Berlin where, showing no symptoms of his later Germanophobia, Balbo politely toasted the president of the German Republic, the German people and German aviation. Finally, the aviators returned to Rome on July 10, completing the 4,000 kilometer tour. Balbo, who should have arrived first in Rome, straggled in fifth. Fortunately for him, there was little publicity about his first attempt to lead such an expedition. Six months afterwards, he brazenly boasted of the cruise."

Soon Balbo, with De Pinedo's assistance, was outlining a second Mediterranean cruise, this time to the east. Segrè provides these details: "Originally, Balbo proposed a flight to Smyrna, Alexandretta and Beirut. The Turkish government denied permission to land in the latter two ports, but it did offer Istanbul. Then, largely by coincidence, a new and daring possibility developed. Through contacts first with two [Russian fleet] officers...and with the Russian Ambassador, Balbo received permission for the expedition to land in Odessa. The final plan ran: Orbetello, Taranto, Athens, Istanbul, Varna (Bulgaria), Odessa...

"The new project was a little longer than the Western Mediterranean cruise about 5,300 kilometers of flying. However, in cost and equipment, the expedition was about half the size of the first...This time the fleet consisted of 32 SM.55s, two S.59bis's and a Cant.22, a total of 35 aircraft and 136 persons. Costs also dictated the timing. The plan was to make the outgoing flight as quickly as possible, and then return in leisurely fashion in order to exploit the publicity aspects to the full. On the return leg, the Italians also planned to do some hard selling: Greece, Turkey, Bulgaria and the Soviet Union were all clients of the Italian aircraft industry.

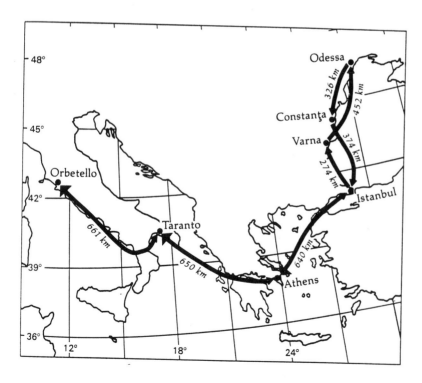

The destination for Balbo's Eastern Mediterranean cruise was Odessa in the Soviet Union. Such cruises, in addition to being impressive publicity stunts, were demanding training missions. Crews trained at Orbetello, a relatively isolated seaplane base built on a peninsula about 150 kilometers north of Rome. There were few distractions, and Balbo was able to drill his men relentlessly. ADAPTED FROM G.B. GUERRI'S *ITALO BALBO*

"In its technical aspects, the expedition proved uneventful—a sign that it had been well prepared. Accidents and mechanical failures were few. A storm, while the expedition was anchored at Constanta, tore three aircraft loose from their moorings, causing enough damage that Balbo postponed departure for a day...

"The real drama of the cruise lay elsewhere: in the meeting with the Soviets in Odessa, and in the bitter rivalry that developed between Balbo and De Pinedo.

"When two ostensibly mortal enemies, communism and fascism, embraced, contradictions and ironies were bound to occur—and they did. The first was the contradiction in the Soviet reception. When the Italian aviators stepped ashore in Odessa, their hosts hailed them as heroes. For the occasion, the Soviets had erected a triumphal arch, built a new wharf, repaired the roads, refurbished two old hotels, and even baked white bread. At the same time, the Soviets kept their visit as secret as possible. On their arrival, the planes were not allowed to approach within ten kilometers of the city. To keep away curious spectators, guards patrolled the hills above the lake where the planes were anchored...During their day-and-a-half visit, the Italians roamed the city as they pleased. When the expedition departed, the authorities inexplicably lifted the ban on flying over the city, and the expedition circled it three times before proceeding toward its destination."

"As a final irony," summarizes Segrè, "the trip to Odessa revealed clearly how Balbo's attitudes toward fascism and toward revolution had changed. His apparent sympathy with his fellow revolutionaries, even if they were Soviets, was polite humbug. Balbo the radical republican had disappeared. On this cruise, as on the previous ones, he mingled easily with royalty, with middle-class statesmen, even with churchmen. In his patriotism, his military courtesies and chivalry, his requisite display of classical culture, he behaved like a traditional Piedmontese general."

As Balbo's assistant chief of staff, De Pinedo grew increasingly critical of his superior. Writes Segrè, "More than once De Pinedo threatened to leave the cruise and return to Italy immediately. Balbo ordered him to stay at his post. De Pinedo obeyed, but he declared that from the moment the expedition reached Italy, Balbo could consider him as having resigned."

Back in Rome, De Pinedo sent the Duce a detailed, blistering critique of the Aeronautica and appealed to Mussolini to appoint him in Balbo's place. Asserts Segrè, "Mussolini did not hesitate in choosing between Balbo and De Pinedo...putting Balbo out of office meant unleashing a dangerous enemy. Moreover, despite De Pinedo's often justified criticisms of Balbo's leadership, Balbo's policies suited Mussolini. Balbo had created a 'fascist service' that popularized the regime."

Unquestionably, the Mediterranean cruises brought prestige to the fascist regime and to Italian aviation. As Segrè notes, "The great powers were forced to take notice of Italy's expansionist aims in the Mediterranean. The cruises may also have helped to sell Italian aircraft, as Balbo claimed, although the connection is less evident. In September 1931, the Turkish government bought twenty-eight Savoia Marchetti flying boats for use against smugglers. The contract was particularly gratifying to the Italians because the Turks had formerly purchased French aircraft...

"The military value of the cruises was more uncertain. Neither Italian nor foreign military experts could fathom the significance of these flights. Paradoxically, they were at the same time swift and mobile, and inflexible and cumbersome. Once in the air, the squadrons moved quickly. However, the preparations, the weather, the refueling and the inability to deviate from their established routes made the flights vulnerable to attack. 'For demonstrations and spectacular effects, the self-contained aerial fleet is naturally more impressive than the same number of aircraft concealed within the walls of an aircraft carrier,' noted an American naval journal. Yet the same aerial fleet operating from a carrier provided far greater range and flexibility.

"For Balbo the cruises had another unpleasant characteristic. They could be used to publicize the fascist regime, but...just as easily to publicize the anti-fascist cause. The success of Balbo's cruises prompted a number of anti-fascists in 1930 and 1931 to undertake daring flights from Switzerland and France in light planes to bombard major Italian cities such as Milan and Rome with propaganda leaflets. The most famous of these attempts was that of the poet Lauro De Bosis in October 1931. Taking off from Marseilles, he succeeded in reaching Rome, showered the city with leaflets, and then disappeared over the sea near Corsica. For Balbo, these flights proved to be an enormous humiliation. His vaunted Aeronautica in those pre-radar days could neither prevent these incursions, nor catch the culprits.

Fortunately for Balbo, De Bosis' feat marked the end of the raids.

"The cruises brought Balbo fame and glory. In 1929, the International League of Aviators offered Balbo the Harmon Trophy. Balbo turned it down, modestly pointing out that he was not in the same league as the previous winners. His contribution had been more as an organizer than as a pilot. He suggested that the trophy be awarded to General Aldo Pellegrini, who had been in charge of the expedition—a slap at De Pinedo. In place of the trophy," Segrè concludes, "Balbo accepted a gold medal of honor."

Mussolini decorates an elated Balbo following one of Balbo's epic flights. Whether the Duce was sincere in his plaudits is still debated. Photo from the U.S. National Archives, College Park, MD

Mussolini's telegram congratulating Balbo on his 1928 aerial cruise read: "You will understand why I waited until you had reached your goal before I sent you my praise and applause for the flight that I willed and that you so superbly carried out. Until everything is finished, nothing is finished." Previously unpublished photo from the U.S. Army Combat Art Collection, Alexandria, VA

Although Balbo fancied himself a great pilot, he once said that his rival Francesco DePinedo was the best pilot in Italy, perhaps the world. "There wasn't room for both of us in the same cockpit," concluded Balbo. DePinedo died when his Belanca ran off the runway at New York's Floyd Bennett Field on September 2, 1933. Overloaded with fuel, the plane burst into flames. Photo from the Caproni Museum Archive, Rome, Italy

Air Marshal Italo Balbo the Aerial Cruise Wizard

"Never, perhaps, as at this moment,
have I felt master of myself."
—Italo Balbo, just prior to his
first Atlantic crossing

In December of 1928 Balbo made his first trip to the U.S. to give a paper at a conference on civil aviation in Washington, D.C. Balbo also visited an aeronautical exposition in Chicago and toured military installations across the U.S. In Dayton, he met Orville Wright, and in Detroit, Henry Ford.

In addition, Balbo inspected the Fleet Air Force on the West Coast. "Technical matters did not interest Balbo," declares Segrè, "but the virtuosity of the American pilots sent him into raptures. After watching six squadrons demonstrate their skills in close formation flying, he declared, 'Their tactical formation was the best I have ever seen.' The organization of the naval air arm also impressed him...

"The trip impressed him deeply. He marveled at the enormous power, wealth and size of the country...[and] was surprised to find that many of the most famous American long-distance flyers had not capitalized on their achievements." As soon as Balbo boarded the *Conte Grande* for home, he began to plan his transatlantic expeditions.

Much of Balbo's fame in international circles was a result of his flights across the Atlantic in 1931 and 1933. The first, across the South Atlantic, was made with fifty men and twelve aircraft. "Balbo flew from Orbetello to Rio de Janeiro, a distance of 10,400 kilometers," writes Segrè. "He lost five men and three aircraft. In men and equipment, this was by far the costliest of the four major cruises...

"One grand vision fired Balbo's Atlantic crossings...'The vision of an Italian aerial squadron, which after having crossed the ocean triumphantly arrived in the sky over New York,' seized his imagination.

"An Atlantic crossing of any sort in those days was a difficult and dangerous enterprise. At that time, there had been forty-seven attempts; only fifteen had succeeded...

"Italians already had two South Atlantic crossings to their credit. De Pinedo with Carlo Del Prete, made the first in 1927 as part of his tour of the Four Continents. The following year, shortly after they set a new world distance record for a closed circuit, Del Prete and Arturo Ferrarin flew 7,450 kilometers nonstop from Rome to Natal in forty-four hours and nine minutes. Balbo chose the banquet in March 1929, in honor of their achievement, to announce, 'We'll cross the Atlantic with various crews as soon as the fight aircraft is available.'...

"The right aircraft turned out, once again, to be the SM.55A, slightly modified. The floats on the new aircraft were larger. The cockpit was completely enclosed and sealed off from the fuel tanks so that the crew could now smoke. The aircraft also had a new, larger engine, the Fiat A 22R, derived from the A 22...The A 22R delivered approximately 200 horsepower more than the Asso 500 and was fitted with new propellers of somewhat larger diameter. The SM.55A had a top speed of 215 km/h, a cruising speed of 165 km/h, and, most important, a range of 3,100 km, about 100 km more than was needed for the longest segment of the flight between Bolama, in Portuguese Guinea on the extreme tip of the West African coast, and Natal, the first stop in Brazil."

Continues Segrè, "Even with the latest aircraft and equipment, the enterprise was full of hazards. Balbo's instrument panel, for instance, would make a modern pilot smile—or perhaps shudder. In the center of the instrument panel, pilot and co-pilot shared various gauges for temperature and pressure of oil, fuel and water. On each side of the instrument panel, pilot and co-pilot had duplicate sets of instruments to control the flight. These included an anemometer or air speed indicator, an altimeter, a variometer or rate-of-climb indicator, an altitude indicator, a gas gauge, and an airflow control for the radiators. At that time, 'blind flying,' flying on instruments alone, was a relatively new technique, but two instruments based on the gyroscope were being developed: artificial horizons supplemented the conventional turn and bank indicators, and directional gyros supplemented the magnetic compasses. Although these instruments were available in 1931, Balbo then described them as 'complicated and very expensive,' and left them off his instrument panel...Balbo's navigational equipment might also strike the contemporary pilot as odd. Balbo's aircraft

Balbo (second from left) visited the Detroit head-quarters of the Ford Motor Company during his first visit to the U.S. in 1928. Henry Ford stands on Balbo's left. Photo from the Caproni Museum Archive, Rome, Italy

Balbo's favorite aircraft and the one in which he made his transoceanic cruises, was the twin-hulled Savoia Marchetti SM.55X flying boat. Here, Balbo (third from left) and fellow Fascist *quadrumvir*, Army Marshal Emilio De Bono (in white goatee), pose on one wing. In *The Pathfinders* David Nevin writes of world reaction to Balbo's daring crossing: "In 1933, a world almost jaded by a surfeit of transoceanic flights was jolted out of its ennui by the spectacle of an entire fleet of Italian planes speeding from Italy to the Chicago World's Fair and back again. The man responsible for this achievement was Italo Balbo, Benito Mussolini's flamboyant minister of air, who had conceived the project to demonstrate the aerial might of fascist Italy." Photo from the U.S. National Archives, College Park, MD

Balbo believed the Regia Aeronautica's frontiers lay "not in individual flights, but in collective cruises of multiple squadrons with no fewer than 80 aircraft. In short," writes Claudio Segrè, "just as he had transformed scattered Blackshirt squads into a militia, now he planned to transmute solo distance and record flights into aerial armadas." In this photo a SM.55X lifts off during a test flight at Orbetello. Photo from the U.S. National Archives, College Park, MD

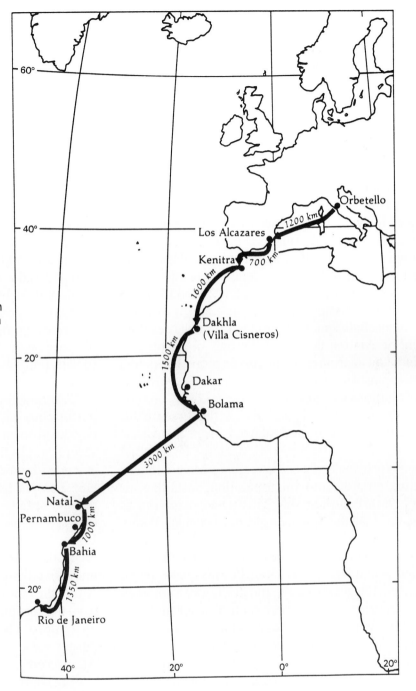

This map outlines Balbo's 1931 South Atlantic cruise route from Italy to Brazil. Adapted from G.B. Guerri's *Italo Balbo*

This cartoon appeared in the December 1993 issue of *Columbus: The Italian-American Magazine* following Balbo's flight to the U.S. A self-satisfied Balbo reports to the Duce: "They gave us everything but rest and sleep."

was literally a flying boat, and he and his crew navigated in the air according to naval techniques and standards. On the little table located in the left float, the navigator laid out his charts, portolans, compasses, chronometers, and sextant and plotted the aircraft's position.

"If the equipment of that era seems rudimentary, the standards for being a good pilot in those days and the style of flying were also vastly different. Today's pilots and astronauts are technicians, sometimes with advanced degrees in engineering or physics. In Balbo's day flying was much more a matter of instinct and of individual heroic achievements. Pilots were judged for their daring and bravery and the elegance of their acrobatic skills. Exhibitionism and bad training took their toll. In Italy, among students of the Accademia Aeronautica between 1923 and 1959, 283 died in war missions, and 426 succumbed to flying accidents. Balbo understood clearly that the development of aviation depended not only on better machines and instruments, but also on more disciplined and sophisticated pilots. He viewed his cruises as contributions to that end.

"From a technical point of view, the success of his first Atlantic expedition depended on one maneuver: the takeoff from Bolama with the large load of fuel necessary to make the ocean crossing. Many complex factors entered into this operation, including air temperature and humidity. Theoretical reassurances that the feat was possible did not convince Balbo. From January to March 1930, Balbo sent Cagna to experiment under the same conditions that the expedition would face a year later. For his crews, Balbo selected thirty-two pilots and thirty-two radiomen and mechanics from the Aeronautica's seaplane units, 'chosen by merit from the moral aristocracy of the Aeronautica.' As their commander he appointed Umberto Maddalena, internationally recognized as a top distance flyer...For a year, beginning January 1, 1930, the crews trained at a seaplane base at Orbetello on the Tyrrhenian coast about 150 kilometers north of Rome.

"The location was ideal. Orbetello was built on a peninsula at the end of which was the promontory of Monte Argentario. The airport was built on a narrow neck of the peninsula between the town and the mainland; large numbers of seaplanes could swing at anchor in the long bay, protected from the sea by a sandbar. Although by air the connection to Rome and its seaplane port of Ostia was easy, Orbetello was relatively isolated by land...Those who trained there

found few worldly distractions—just as Balbo had planned. Orbetello was to be no ordinary training base. He spoke of it a quasi-religious community...

"The training was tough and at times costly. The men were given leave only once every two weeks. They became proficient in both the academic and practical disciplines. For example, they learned celestial navigation—perhaps far more than they needed. Such skills had been necessary for such solo flights like those of De Pinedo in 1927 and Del Prete in 1928. They had braved the Atlantic without radios or a system of support that advised them of their positions. Balbo's expeditions had both—a measure of how much more complex and sophisticated his expedition was, and of how quickly aviation technology changed. Balbo also put his men through a long series of training flights. These included night flights, take-offs with progressively heavier loads, and flights of up to twenty hours, the time necessary to cover the distance on the longest leg of the flight. The training took its toll. Two died on November 27 while practicing...

"Although he spent much of his time in Rome performing his duties as minister, Balbo did not neglect his own training. During July 1930, he spent several weeks literally camping in a pine grove that extended between Viareggio and Forte dei Marmi. He...also put in flying hours and looked in on the training at Orbetello. Like any pilot, he had his share of near-fatal accidents. One of the worst came in June 1930...While taking off near Capri, one of the floats on his seaplane gave way and the plane sank almost immediately to a depth of more than twelve meters. Although injured, Balbo managed to free himself from the cockpit and surfaced after he had been given up for dead. The incident haunted him; he recalled it during some of the worst moments of his North Atlantic crossing in 1933.

"In choosing his route across the South Atlantic, Balbo followed the trail of earlier pioneers. The first stop, Los Alcazares, Spain, had been the furthest point for the first Mediterranean cruise in 1928. The ports along the west coast of Africa—Kenitra, Morocco, Villa Cisneros, Rio de Oro (today Dakhla, Mauritania); Bolama, Portuguese Guinea (today Guinea Bissau)—had all been utilized by De Pinedo and Del Prete in 1927, or by other conquerors of the south Atlantic, such as the French aviator Jean Mermoz.

"By mid-December of 1930, the expedition was ready. It comprised four squadrons of three planes each, with two aircraft in reserve. The crews totaled fifty-six, with twelve in reserve. Balbo had begun with the more modest ambition of only two squadrons totaling six, but when Mussolini assured him that the expedition would work with larger numbers, Balbo cheerfully doubled its size. He moved to Orbetello on December 9 and officially took command of the expedition on December 14. 'The greatest formation flight in the history of flying'...was about to begin."

"The first leg of the expedition from Orbetello to Los Alcazares nearly turned into a disaster," Segrè relates. "For two days, Balbo postponed the departure because of the weather. Finally, on December 17, the weather was 'not at all prohibitive,' Balbo wrote. One cyclone had passed across their route, but another one was forming. Had he postponed his departure another twenty-four hours, he would have had perfect weather. Inexperience, impatience and the pressures of well-wishers and journalists who crowded around Orbetello all contributed to Balbo's faulty judgment. From Orbetello across the Tyrrhenian and through the passage between Sardegna and Corsica, the weather held. Shortly afterwards, for about two hours, the fourteen seaplanes 'engaged in a life and death struggle' with the storm. Fierce rains threatened to rip the fabric covering off the wings. Visibility was close to zero. Down drafts swept Balbo's aircraft from an altitude of two or three hundred meters to just above the wave caps. The radios no longer worked. To maintain some semblance of formation, Balbo ordered his mechanic to peer out the portholes and shout course directions. Nevertheless, Balbo lost track of time and of the rest of the expedition. Five aircraft remained with him; eight flew off to the north. Fortunately, at this point he saw land below—the Balearic Islands. Eventually he and the five aircraft with him landed in the little bay of Puerto de Campo, a fishing village of three hundred people. He had saved half his expedition. He did not learn until late in the afternoon, when he managed to contact Rome by radio, that the rest of the aircraft had landed safely in Los Alcazares. For forty-eight hours, the storm lashed the island. Not until December 19 was Balbo able to rejoin Maddalena and the others. In the primitive lodgings, in wet, cold and humid weather, Balbo developed a fever that plagued him for several days afterwards.

"The expedition had been saved, and the aircraft were not seriously damaged; however, the rain and hail had pitted and scarred the wooden propellers. At Los Alcazares, new ones were fitted, but there were not enough for the entire expedition. Those that could not be replaced remained unbalanced. For the rest of the expedition, they vibrated and thus put unusual stress on the engines.

"This near disaster raised doubts in Mussolini's mind about the leadership of the expedition. Even today it is not clear where the responsibility lies for the original error in misjudging the weather: with the weather service, with the expedition's collective leadership, with Balbo himself. The error might have been rectified after the expedition took off, for the storm worsened by stages. The expedition might easily have returned to Orbetello or even to Elmas (on Sardinia) before the situation became critical. The wear and tear on the aircraft, especially on the propellers, could have been avoided. Either Balbo or Maddalena could have given the order. There is no evidence of radio messages between the two. Maddalena plunged ahead. His stubbornness and determination might have been appropriate for a race or a solo flight, but not for such an expedition. Balbo, who was not nearly as experienced a pilot, trusted Maddalena's judgment. Balbo redeemed himself a bit when he chose to land at Puerto de Camp, but already Mussolini's confidence in Balbo may have been shaken. The Duce withheld his congratulatory telegram until the very end of the expedition when he could be certain that the cruise had ended successfully.

"On December 21 the expedition resumed, hopping along the northwest coast of Africa from Los Alcazares to Bolama, where they arrived on Christmas Day. For the next twelve days Balbo and his men prepared for the critical flight across the Atlantic. The question on everyone's mind was always the takeoff. Fuel, crew, oil, water, supplies and food totaled 4,700 kilograms. In addition, there was the weight of the SM.55 itself. Listed as 5,200 kilograms, after three weeks of soaking in the water, the wooden frame was considerably heavier.

"Thus, the engines had to lift a total of 9,900 kilograms. On prior Atlantic crossings in equatorial zones, 1,000-horsepower seaplanes had lifted only two-thirds that much weight. On January 2, Maddalena and Cagna, during the hottest hours of the day and with no wind, lifted off after a run of eighty-five seconds and landed safely again. Balbo planned to leave at night. At a lower temperature the task would be much easier. Nevertheless, to increase the safety margin, he ordered everything feasible done to lighten the load, including jettisoning the rubber life rafts. In case of emergency, the pilots were to stay with their planes to the last moment, to defend their craft as if they were defending their own lives, 'but to consider themselves lost at the moment in which the aircraft was lost.'

"Balbo also waited patiently—after his experience during the first leg of the journey—for the most favorable weather. On this—the longest and most difficult part of the trip—the expedition would fly 3,000 kilometers, from Bolama to Porto Natal. He estimated the flying time at about twenty hours. Since part of the flight had to be at night, he wanted to take advantage of the moonlight and the trade winds. From a study of the past weather records, January 4 at 11:30 P.M.. appeared to be the ideal date; three times—January 2, 3, 4—he postponed. On January 5, the weather improved a bit. With no guarantee that it would get any better and afraid of losing the moonlight, he set the departure for 1:30 A.M.

"That evening the sunset was dark and the sky was overcast. Night came on with a heavy, leaden hue. The moon was veiled behind a thick layer of clouds. Originally, Balbo had planned for only a dozen planes to make the flight. The two reserve pilots, however, convinced Balbo to include them. Emotions ran high. Aboard the yacht *Alice*, one of the support ships, Balbo's excitement mounted as each succeeding crew boarded...He played an aimless card game until the last crew member was aboard the last aircraft. By then the moon had disappeared entirely and it was impossible to distinguish between water and sky.

"At exactly 1:29 Greenwich time, Balbo was in the cockpit of his own aircraft carrying the special civil registration I-BALB, ready for takeoff. 'I am very calm. My nerves are submissive to the will that controls them. Never, perhaps, as at this moment, have I felt master of myself.' With everyone ready, 'into the unknown and toward the unknown we launch the aircraft at full speed.' The enormous seaplane, so heavy that the stern was almost entirely underwater, rose abruptly out of the dense water. Faster and faster it sliced through the waves, lifted up on the step. With all their strength, Balbo and Cagna pulled the stick back against their chests. At this moment of top speed, 'woe if you look out of the cockpit toward the surface of the water. Woe if you look for the horizon. The slightest indecision, the slightest hesitation...guarantees the loss of life and aircraft. Forward, forward straight into the dark.' At last they felt the aircraft break from the surface and rush up into the night sky. For the next twenty minutes, in total darkness, their eyes glued to the altimeter, they climbed in a straight line without losing speed until Balbo nudged, 'We're safe.'

"The rest of the expedition was less fortunate. Balbo, first in the air, could not follow what was happening. I-VALL, which was part of his immediate squadron, had trouble lifting off, he knew, because of an overheated motor. The other squadrons took to the sky without incident, except for the I-RECA, which like I-VALL, suffered from overheating. About twelve minutes after takeoff, while the crews of the two aircraft waited for their motors to cool off, they saw a great flash and glow on the horizon in the direction that the expedition had taken. It was I-BOER. The plane exploded and sank. No trace of the aircraft or of the crew was ever found. The cause of the explosion was never determined. Balbo blamed a short circuit in the electrical system.

"At 3 A.M., I-VALL and I-RECA, their motors cooled, attempted another takeoff. I-VALL gained cruising altitude without incident. I-RECA, maneuvering to keep I-VALL in sight, lost airspeed. The big seaplane hit the water, smashing the right float and killing the mechanic who was riding there. In all, during the night in Bolama, five crewmen and two aircraft were lost.

"For the first six hours of the flight, Balbo's nerves were on edge; then the tension eased. After daybreak, the flight became routine except for the need to maintain formation. For eighteen hours the pilots constantly adjusted their engine speeds and maneuvered to maintain their positions in the flight. In exasperation, Balbo the archenemy of solo flights became their great booster. 'I think that if I were to do another Atlantic flight, I would prefer to do it three times from one end to the other solo rather than once again in formation,' he wrote.

"Only two more incidents marred the flight. At low altitudes the heat of the day made it difficult for the radiators to cool the engines adequately. The mechanics found themselves using all the available liquids aboard—water, drinks, even urine. I-BAIS and I-DONA eventually succumbed to overheating and landed in mid-ocean. A support ship attempted to tow I-BAIS to the mainland, but eventually the aircraft sank—the third loss of the expedition. I-DONA was saved and rejoined the cruise at Natal.

"At 20 hours Greenwich time (5 P.M. local time) the main body of the expedition, nine aircraft, reached

Natal. They had crossed in about eighteen and a half hours at an average speed of 162 km/h. I-VALL, flying solo, took seventeen hours and averaged 177 km/h. Balbo's complaints about the difficulties of formation flying were confirmed.

"Natal welcomed the aviators with the peal of the city's church bells...In Italy, the expedition's safe arrival stirred patriotic celebrations. Mussolini personally made the announcement to the king. Performances at La Scala in Milan and the Teatro Reale dell'Opera in Rome were interrupted to announce the good news.

"A tidal wave of congratulatory telegrams from all over the world swept into Balbo's hotel room. 'They scare me—I can't escape them.' From Italy alone there were more than two thousand, from everyone from the king to D'Annunzio. From Mussolini, however, there was nothing...

"For five days the expedition stayed in Natal," continues Segrè, "then on January 11 they flew to Bahia, where huge crowds of Italian immigrants greeted the aviators. Balbo planned the expedition's last leg, the grand entry into Rio de Janeiro on January 15, carefully. The expedition arrived early and circled outside the harbor for about an hour. The magic moment came precisely at 4:30 P.M. The entire expedition, ships and aircraft, entered the harbor simultaneously. The triumphant *atlantici* in a V-formation, with Balbo in the lead, soared above the eight support ships into 'the golden sky of the great metropolis.' It was a sight worthy of the greatest Italian painters...Balbo rhapsodized...'Forward, forward winged squadron of Italy. After the run over the ocean, you have earned this scene of beauty and fantasy. Follow me faithfully. In the skies of Rio we'll trace an aerial wreath of joy, of strength, of friendship.'

"The expedition touched down, taxied to the anchoring buoys, and shut off the engines. The crews climbed out onto the wings of their aircraft and stood at attention. From the eight ships came the first of nineteen salvos from their forty-eight guns. Salutes from Brazilian warships and nearby forts joined in the chorus...Balbo disembarked under an avalanche of flowers...'That day, descending from the sky, covered with glory, he stood straight as a sword and he radiated joy,' a friend remarked.

"One of his first acts that afternoon was to make a radio broadcast to North America. Now that the great South American enterprise had concluded, he declared, he wanted very much to carry out another one across the North Atlantic to bring greetings from the Fatherland to the Italians in the United States. He also found a telegram from Mussolini...

"For three weeks Balbo remained in Brazil, visiting the Italian immigrant communities in Rio and São Paulo. On February 7 he sailed for Italy. On his return he received a tumultuous welcome and made a series of public appearances in major Italian cities. He was rewarded with the nation's gold medal for military valor. Two honors, however, escaped him. He was made neither a count nor a marshal ...Mussolini...decided against ennobling Balbo...As for Balbo's aspirations to become an air marshal, 'The President [Mussolini],' De Bono commented, 'got a little annoyed. These youngsters have no sense of proportion.' Balbo was in a 'bad mood and discontented,' he added.

"If Balbo did not receive all the accolades he wanted at home, abroad he emerged as one of the giants of the flying world. The International Federation of Aviators awarded him its gold medal for the finest aeronautical undertaking of the year. He had joined the company of De Pinedo, who had won it when it was first given in 1925, and Lindbergh, who received it in 1927. In London and Paris the leading lights of the flying world praised his feat...The foreign press was warm in its praise. 'A Great Flight' and 'Well Done, Italy,' commented two English papers...The only negative comment was some surprise in the foreign papers that in Italy the news of the death of the five aviators in Bolama was withheld for two days, until January 8. It was, concluded the English press, in order not to mar the celebrations over the triumph. Balbo, infuriated, declared that the delay was purely for the sake of accuracy—to be sure that there was no hope for the aviators—and out of respect for the families of the dead."

Concludes Segrè, "In the meantime, he had already turned his attention to his new project. From the moment he had arrived in Rio de Janeiro, he made clear that the flight to Brazil was only a stepping stone to a larger enterprise."

Just two months after his return to Italy, Balbo had crews in training at Orbetello for a second crossing. Initially he proposed that a fleet circle the globe. The Sino-Japanese War and the capital required for such a trip made the idea unfeasible, but some of the grandeur was maintained in a plan to cross the North Atlantic and to visit the Century of Progress Fair in Chicago.

"In the past," writes Segrè, "Balbo had chosen

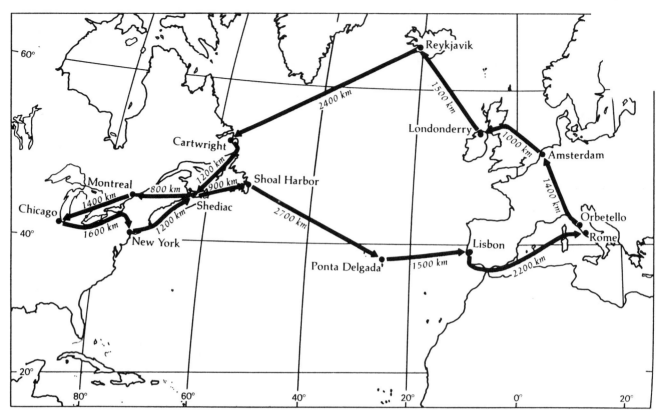

This is the North American cruise route. Balbo's final cruise of 1933.

pilots from among those who were already familiar with seaplanes. For this cruise, to broaden the experience of his men, he selected seventy officers of whom four-fifths had no experience with these aircraft. However, he also included about a dozen veterans of the expedition to Brazil; they provided experience and inspired the younger pilots. The academic program included courses in mathematics, physics, aerodynamics, thermodynamics, navigation, and English. The practical program included flying an average of five hundred hours over two years. The men also worked on their sailing skills, for once on the water, their aircraft became an unwieldy boat. The movements of wind and waves, the fundamentals of handling a small boat, the problems of taxing up to buoys and then tying up, and the transfer of men and materials at sea were all vital to handling their aircraft. Since the expedition would venture to extreme northern latitudes the crews trained in snow and ice in Misurina during the winter of 1932/33. To practice

formation flying, they flew a series of missions throughout the Mediterranean. Discipline was harsh. Thirty-five of the original applicants failed and were replaced," notes Segrè.

"The rigorous training, combined with Balbo's minute planning, paid off. The discipline never dimmed the enthusiasm of the pilots and crews. On the eve of their departure, they felt completely confident in their skills, their machines, and their organization...On their return from Chicago, they felt capable of starting regular service across the North Atlantic. Due to the careful training and preparation, Balbo lost only two aircraft and two crew members during the 1933 double crossing. This was an impressive achievement. In the previous crossings, all one-way, twenty-seven out of forty-five aircraft had been lost, with twenty-three deaths.

"Balbo methodically organized his logistical support and his weather service. The expedition was promoted as an Italian effort...Much of the crucial

Fascist Eagle

support, however, was international, beginning with an international congress of transoceanic aviators that Balbo convened in Rome in May 1932. Balbo used the occasion to show off the Aeronautica. The guests toured the new ministry building and attended demonstrations and rallies that, according to one visitor, made the 'vaunted Broadway Parade fade into insignificance.'...About the same time, he sent pilots on three separate missions to scout possible landing sites from Labrador and Newfoundland to Greenland and Iceland. On the basis of their reports," explains Segrè, "he planned a route that would touch on Iceland and Labrador on the initial crossing and would return via Newfoundland and Ireland. Accurate weather information was crucial to the success of the expedition. National weather service that covered the path of this flight—Italian, German, Danish, English, Canadian and American—all contributed to the effort. He also established special weather centers...The International Telephone and Telegraph Co. donated radio links among the weather centers, the bases, and the squadron. Balbo also stationed eleven weather ships along the flight path."

David Nevin adds this information in *The Pathfinders*: "On the ground, servicing equipment had to be positioned and monumental supplies of fuel stockpiled at stopovers. To radio reports of the latest weather, a chain of six trawlers had to be strung across the Atlantic."

As for the aircraft, "Once again," states Segrè, "Balbo chose the tough, durable Savoia Marchetti SM.55—a flying machine, as he pointed out, that had given the Italians a total of fifteen Atlantic crossings. The SM.55X model (the X did not stand for 'experimental,' but was a Roman numeral for the Decennial cruise) was a refinement of the one he had used on the first Atlantic cruise. The most important change was in the engines. Fiat A.22R engines had powered the earlier SM.55TA model. Balbo wanted larger engines. A competition developed between the Fiat A.24R, developed from the Schneider engines, and the Isotta Fraschini Asso 11R. Both engines were rated at 750 horsepower...Balbo...declared that he would choose on the basis of test performance. After a test of 500 hours, the Isotta Fraschini won. The SM.55X had a top speed of 280 km/h, a cruising speed of 225 km/h, and a range of more than 4,000 kilometers. There were other refinements: larger fuel tanks, modified radiators, metal propellers, and more sophisticated instruments."

Notes Segrè, "By the beginning of May 1933, preparations for the expedition were nearly complete...Everything now depended on the weather...from mid-June to the first of July storms buffeted the Alps and northcentral Europe almost continuously. For nearly two weeks, Balbo and his crews waited anxiously...

"Finally, during the night of June 30 to July 1, the weather cleared...Following a flag-raising ceremony

Balbo's armada of Savoia Marchetti SM.55X seaplanes line up at anchor at Orbetello before the epic July 1933 Decennial Cruise to North America. Just four months later, in November, the Duce relieved Balbo of command of the Aeronautica and sent him to reign as governor of Libya. Photo from the U.S. National Archives, College Park, MD

Part of Balbo's 75 seaplane armada anchors on the waters of Lake Michigan along the Chicago sea wall following their 9,700 kilometer journey from Italy. En route the pilots faced great fog banks, a challenge, Balbo reported "always produces one effect for sure: my heart jumps into my mouth." PHOTO FROM THE U.S. NATIONAL ARCHIVES, COLLEGE PARK, MD at dawn, Balbo gave the order for departure...By 4:37 Balbo's own I-BALB was in the air and by 5:00 the entire expedition was airborne...

"The aerial armada roared northward in formation: eight flights of three aircraft apiece. The twenty-fifth plane was considered a reserve and assigned to the eighth flight...As with the flight to Brazil, whenever weather permitted, Balbo maintained the formation, both for discipline and for show.

"On that first day, Saturday, July 1, the expedition soared over the Alps in a majestic formation that was widely reproduced in photographs, on postcards and even on a book jacket. After a seven-hour flight, the aviators reached Amsterdam...Sixty Dutch aircraft rose to meet them...The boats in the landing area constituted a major hazard for the twenty-five pilots trying to set down their aircraft; but in the first fatal accident, which occurred here, pilot error rather than the harbor traffic was ruled the cause. The pilot of I-DINI overshot his landing and flipped over. Three of the crew and a passenger were saved; a fourth crewman died, trapped in the wreckage."

"With their aircraft safely anchored...," notes Segrè, "Balbo and his men faced the second major challenge of their arrival: the public ceremonies and festivities...In Amsterdam, however, out of respect for their dead comrade, Balbo ordered all festivities...suspended...

"The following day, Sunday, July 2, in five and a half hours the expedition crossed the North Sea, flew over Newcastle, Edinburgh, and Glasgow, and landed in Londonderry, Ireland. Howling winds at their next destination, Reykjavik, Iceland, delayed the expedition. Finally, on July 5, the four weather ships, stationed at 340-kilometer intervals along the route signaled favorable conditions...As the temperature dropped toward freezing, the aviators watched nervously for ice forming on the wings. Then, abruptly, they emerged into clear weather. By six o'clock that evening, at the end of their 1,528-kilometer flight, they were tying up in the harbor at Reykjavik. They stepped into a subpolar cold of 5 degrees Centigrade. For the first time they appreciated the value of their Alpine training—and their fur-lined overcoats and hats.

"For the next six days the expedition remained...waiting for the weather to clear and preparing for the second and most difficult stage of the North Atlantic crossing: from Reykjavik to Cartwright, Labrador...The weather had to be right...

"At last, on Wednesday, July 12, the expedition roared off again into skies filled with fog and rain...In contrast to flying over land, flying over water, [Balbo] fretted...The hours, especially the last ones, dragged on like months...Showers of rain battered the aircraft and water leaked into the cockpit...Visions of the ocean engulfing him again, as it had almost two years ago at Capri, haunted him...

"At last, at seven o'clock in the evening, after twelve hours in the air, the expedition reached the coffee-colored waters of Sandwich Bay. They had covered 2,400 kilometers...their discipline was so tight that on arrival there were no stragglers. Each flight of three arrived at the same time and in the same position they had occupied during takeoff...

"Fatigue lay heavily on pilots and crews the next day, but they flew for six hours in excellent weather from Cartwright to Shediac, Newfoundland...On Friday, July 14, the expedition flew from Shediac to Montreal in five hours...

"On Saturday, July 15, at about 5:45 P.M. local Chicago time, a boy with binoculars first sighted them...The crowds that lined the shores of Lake Michigan...went 'wild with joy; Italians among them nearly burst.' 'Viva Italia!' 'Viva Balbo!' Two weeks after they had left Orbetello, Balbo's armada was in the skies over Chicago. Their elapsed flying time had been forty-eight hours and forty-seven minutes. They had flown 9,766 kilometers (6,065 miles) at an average of 200 km/h (124.6 mph)."

Balbo and his men received a hearty welcome. The mayor proclaimed "Balbo Day" and Seventh Street was renamed "Balbo Avenue." Everywhere Balbo was lionized, even inducted into the Sioux tribe as Chief Flying Eagle.

On July 19, reports Segrè, the expedition flew to New York. "Millions waved and cheered as the armada flew over Manhattan and landed at the Coney Island seaplane base...Nowhere in Italy or Europe had he seen anything like New York and its crowds." The next day Balbo lunched at the White House with President Franklin D. Roosevelt. Later he met fellow aviator Wiley Post, who, writes Segrè, claimed that "Italian aviation was leading the world."

Watching from Rome, Mussolini grew increasingly jealous over Balbo's grand welcome in the U.S. "The flight was not a mere sporting event, he chided, and he urged Balbo to minimize the party-going and festivities...Balbo prudently turned down offers to extend the expedition to other parts of the United States and Canada. Then, hoping to entice Balbo to return quickly to Italy, Mussolini dangled the big

Chicago Mayor Edward J. Kelly (left) presents Balbo with a key to the city. In addition, Kelly proclaimed July 15, 1933, "Italo Balbo Day" and renamed 7th Avenue "Balbo Avenue," the name it retains to this day. PHOTO FROM THE U.S. NATIONAL ARCHIVES, COLLEGE PARK, MD

Escorted by American police officers, Balbo (center) is welcomed to the Chicago World's Fair by young Italian-American women. PHOTO FROM THE U.S. NATIONAL ARCHIVES, COLLEGE PARK, MD

Ever the showman, Balbo dons a Sioux Indian headdress for a colorful photo opportunity. At left is the presenter, Chief Evergreen Tree. PHOTO FROM THE U.S. NATIONAL ARCHIVES, COLLEGE PARK, MD

Balbo's transatlantic cruise made headline news across the United States. The expedition landed in New York City on July 19, 1933. FROM THE CAPRONI MUSEUM ARCHIVE, ROME, ITALY

Famous Italian athletes salute Balbo, "Sportsman of the Air," in this period cartoon that appeared in the December 1933 edition of *Columbus: The Italian-American Magazine*. Although critics denied that Balbo's expedition had military significance, Claudio Segrè notes that Gen. William Mitchell stated that the flight "revealed how this country [the U.S.] is allowing foreign nations to outstrip her in air forces."

This advertisement featuring Balbo appeared in the August 1933 edition of *Aero Digest*. COURTESY *AERO DIGEST*

Mussolini (right) enthusiastically greets Balbo after Balbo's return from North America in 1933. PHOTO FROM THE CAPRONI MUSEUM ARCHIVE, ROME, ITALY

Balbo's aerial armada receives a tumultuous welcome at Ostia outside Rome upon his return from North America. According to Claudio Segrè, "Balbo viewed this expedition as a pioneering step toward commercial flights across the Atlantic. The cruise also served the usual publicity and propagandistic purposes. Even in 1933, in the depths of the Depression exported from the United States, Fascist Italy was vital and resilient—this was the intended message of Balbo's expedition." PHOTO FROM THE U.S. NATIONAL ARCHIVES, COLLEGE PARK, MD

August 13, 1933: By permitting them to parade under the Roman Arch of Constantine upon their return from the successful North Atlantic crossing, the Duce accorded the *atlantici* a great honor. Balbo (center), clutching his dress sword at his side, salutes while his archenemy, Achille Starace, wearing Fascist Blackshirt uniform at right, gives the Roman salute. PHOTO FROM THE CAPRONI MUSEUM ARCHIVES, ROME, ITALY

Despite this hug at the Lido di Roma and a marshal's baton from the Duce upon his return from his North Atlantic flight, Balbo knew well of Mussolini's jealousy. Balbo and fellow pilots are dressed in aviators' whites. PHOTO FROM THE U.S. NATIONAL ARCHIVES, COLLEGE PARK, MD

July 20, 1940: Dino Alfieri, the Duce's Ambassador to Germany, poses with Edda Göring during a tea party held at Göring's country estate. Alfieri survived WWII and published his memoirs in 1954. He writes: "Mussolini did all he could to encourage the project of the Atlantic cruise, ingeniously conceived and superbly organized by Balbo, because he saw in it a particularly effective propaganda stunt calculated to bring worldwide prestige both to Fascist Italy and to himself. He ordered a magnificent reception to be prepared for Balbo and his fellow aviators on their return, insisted on welcoming them personally, and made arrangements for them to pass in triumph beneath the Arch of Constantine, but, when it seemed to him that Balbo's attitude was becoming a shade too peremptory and independent, when his sycophants repeated to him—skillfully garbled—various remarks which might have been interpreted as criticisms of certain Fascist methods and even of their leader, Mussolini decided to remove him from Italy—in particular, from Rome—and to pack him off to the Colonies, and so he appointed him Governor of Libya."
PREVIOUSLY UNPUBLISHED PHOTO FROM THE HERMANN GÖRING ALBUMS IN THE LIBRARY OF CONGRESS, WASHINGTON, D.C.

carrot. His telegram hinted that he would award Balbo the baton of an air marshal upon his return. In the past, only major heroes of the Great War, generals Armando Diaz, Luigi Cadorna, and Pietro Badoglio, and Admiral Thaon di Revel had been so rewarded," explains Segrè. "In the fledgling Aeronautica, the rank did not exist."

Balbo initiated the return on July 25. The planes landed first in Nova Scotia, then in Newfoundland. The plan was to cross to Valentia, Ireland, but bad weather forced Balbo to consider other routes. "Mussolini," relates Segrè, "bombarded him with 'suggestions' based on his instincts as a 'country weatherman,' as he labeled himself. The 'suggestions,' however, had more to do with politics than with the weather. Mussolini did not want Balbo to set down in London, Paris or Berlin on his return...Finally, Mussolini sent orders directly: until August 10 the expedition was to aim for Ireland; after that date, the Azores.

"Balbo made his own decision. On August 8, the expedition took off for the Azores. The crossing took place without incident. Nine of the aircraft landed at Horta and fifteen at Ponta Delgada. The following day, however, the second fatality of the trip occurred. I-RANI, in taking off from Ponta Delgrada, overturned. Lieutenant Enrico Squaglia, one of the pilots, was fatally injured. The cause of the accident was never determined...

"On Saturday, August 12, Balbo led his men on the last leg of the journey, from Lisbon to the Lido di Roma, a distance of more than 2,200 kilometers...

"An ecstatic crowd, including Mussolini and members of the royal family, and a bombastic welcome awaited the heroes. The moment Balbo stepped ashore, Mussolini, in a rapid, spontaneous movement, embraced him affectionately and kissed him on both cheeks. 'In this gesture he says everything to me and I everything to him,' declared Balbo. But Mussolini had more: a triumphant march under the Arch of Constantine...A triumphant motorcade bore the heroes...to Piazza Venizia and Piazzo Colonna in downtown Rome, a journey that took about an hour. Four huge searchlights lighted up Piazzo Colonna as bright as day. The crowds demonstrated joyously while the *atlantici* waved from a balcony. Above them was a huge mural showing the route of the expedition. White lamps marked the outbound voyage; red the return. Above the map was a huge portrait of Mussolini...

"In Rome it was difficult to tell whether it was Balbo or Mussolini who had flown the Atlantic. Great posters displayed Mussolini in aviator's costume beside a squadron of planes, as if he'd done the flying and Balbo had assisted him...

"The cruise came to a formal conclusion...when the expedition flew from Ostia to their base at Orbetello for a last presentation to the king. Afterwards, Balbo embraced each member of the expedition individually and departed...

"The expedition had been an enormous success, far greater than he had anticipated. Under normal odds, only twenty of the twenty-four aircraft would have completed the trip. How to account for such success? Careful organization, training, careful quality control over the equipment...

"Did the cruise prove that regular airline service was possible? The North Atlantic was still too tough for regular commercial air service, he concluded. Temporary flights between Iceland and Labrador during the summer were feasible as long as the weather was good; the central route between the Azores and Bermuda might also work during the winter. For the moment, however, he did not see regular service as a possibility."

"From the perspective of half a century, how does Balbo's evaluation stand up?" asks Segrè. "Technically, the cruise was a grand achievement...Balbo had beaten the odds. Moreover, as he pointed out, his Atlantic expeditions were in a class by themselves. They were not sporting adventures that depended on an exceptional pilot with exceptional courage and skills. Like the space flights of today, Balbo's Atlantic cruises proved the value of organization, method, routine. They marked a watershed between the pioneering-sporting phases of aviation and the new commercial-industrial era...

"In addition to its technical brilliance, the flight promised to make a major contribution to the development of commercial aviation...By the late 1940s, about fifty years ahead of Balbo's estimate of the year 2000, regular commercial air traffic across the North Atlantic became a reality."

Did the cruise actually detract from the military effectiveness of the Aeronautica? Asserts Segrè, "The training that his men received at Orbetello was first-class and Italian pilots gained a world wide reputation for their excellence. Whether this cruise, or any of the others provided effective training for the organization of the whole is another matter. Balbo claimed that he was not training an elite. This was nonsense. The seventy or so *atlantici* who trained

Göring's visit to Italy
January 16, 1937

January 16, 1937: Göring and high-ranking Italian and German officers observe a fly-by upon Göring's arrival at Guidonia Airport. PREVIOUSLY UNPUBLISHED PHOTO FROM THE HERMANN GÖRING ALBUMS IN THE LIBRARY OF CONGRESS, WASHINGTON, D.C.

German Luftwaffe Col. Gen. Hermann Göring alights from an SM.79 in Italy. The German officer holding Göring's dress sword is aide Col. Bernd von Brauchitsch. PREVIOUSLY UNPUBLISHED PHOTO FROM THE HERMANN GÖRING ALBUMS IN THE LIBRARY OF CONGRESS, WASHINGTON, D.C.

Göring (carrying dress sword) and an entourage of German and Italian air force officers depart from the air ministry building in Rome. PREVIOUSLY UNPUBLISHED PHOTO FROM THE HERMANN GÖRING ALBUMS IN THE LIBRARY OF CONGRESS, WASHINGTON, D.C.

Göring's visit to Balbo's Air Ministry Building in Rome April 10, 1933

April 10, 1933: Göring (second from left) makes a point to Balbo (right) through an interpreter, while Luftwaffe Gen. Erhard Milch (left) looks on. Despite his rapport with Göring, Balbo remained adamantly opposed to an Italian-German military or political alliance. PREVIOUSLY UNPUBLISHED PHOTO FROM THE HERMANN GÖRING ALBUMS IN THE LIBRARY OF CONGRESS, WASHINGTON, D.C.

April 10, 1933: A bust of the Duce in aviator's cap and goggles in the air ministry building provides a backdrop for this photo of Balbo (left) and Göring, thinking him "flashy and pretentious." (A classic case of the pot calling the kettle black!) The Duce also did not approve of his [Göring's] admiration of Balbo. PREVIOUSLY UNPUBLISHED PHOTO FROM THE HERMANN GÖRING ALBUMS IN THE LIBRARY OF CONGRESS, WASHINGTON, D.C.

at Orbetello for two years were no more 'ordinary' than pioneering astronauts in a space program. Balbo liked to boast of his 3,100 pilots, yet only seventy were admitted to the Orbetello course and about one hundred men, pilots and crews, flew with the expedition. Balbo pointed out that after the expeditions, the *atlantici* were distributed widely throughout the ranks of the Aeronautica. They shared their experiences and served as an inspiration to their fellow airmen. Perhaps they did. Nevertheless, such a procedure seems an odd substitute for training the organization as a whole...

"What Balbo had shown was the Douhet's facile dreams of irresistible aerial fleets were difficult to achieve in practice. Aerial fleets might be possible, but they required a long period of preparation and practice. On the other hand, to charge that Balbo's cruises were somehow responsible for Italy's lack of preparation in World War II is absurd."

Both Chicago's Balbo Avenue and its monument to the transatlantic crossing survived World War II and anti-fascist sentiment, although Segrè relates this postwar incident. "The Italian Ambassador to the United States, Alberto Tarchiani, a militant anti-fascist, requested that these tributes be removed. Reportedly, the mayor of Chicago was surprised at the request and replied, 'Why? Didn't Balbo cross the Atlantic?'"

Segrè concludes with this bit of irony. "After World War II, memory of the flight that was intended to publicize fascism was revived as a symbol of Italian-American friendship. For the twentieth anniversary of the flight in 1953, the American air attaché organized a banquet in Rome for the surviving *atlantici*. The fortieth anniversary celebrations in 1973 were even more impressive; fifty-eight of the surviving members of the expedition and Balbo's son Paolo flew to Chicago for the city's annual Columbus Day celebration. As they had forty years earlier, the *atlantici* paraded triumphantly through the streets...before cheering crowds estimated at 10,000...Most moving of all to the veterans of the cruise was the reaction of the Italian-American community. Many families had treasured programs and other souvenirs from the original flight. In 1973, the *atlantici* found a new generation, waving the memorabilia of forty years earlier, once again clamoring for autographs."

A trophy won by Balbo's Aeronautica is displayed during Göring's visit to Italy in the spring of 1933. Balbo was at the peak of his career when suddenly, that fall, he fell afoul of Mussolini's jealously and was asked to resign from the Aeronautica. The Duce even ordered the Aeronautica purged of Balbo's influence. "Balbisti in the Aeronautica were 'suspected and persecuted,'" writes Claudio Segrè. "On one of Balbo's first visits to Italy after assuming his position in Tripoli, not a single representative of the air ministry was at the train station in Rome to greet him." PREVIOUSLY UNPUBLISHED PHOTO FROM THE HERMANN GÖRING ALBUMS IN THE LIBRARY OF CONGRESS, WASHINGTON, D.C.

Italians await the arrival of Nazi Propaganda Minister Dr. Josef Goebbels at an airfield outside Rome in 1933. Fascist party secretary Achille Starace stands at far left; Balbo peers over a shoulder. Starace never got along with Balbo. In the words of Dino Alfieri: "Cleverly handled and egged on by the party secretary, Starace...Ciano easily became an enemy of Balbo. Superficially their relations were amicable, but Ciano let slip no opportunity of disparaging Balbo's work, whether in political circles, among diplomats, in the presence of his father-in-law, or in Roman drawing rooms." PREVIOUSLY UNPUBLISHED PHOTO FROM THE HEINRICH HOFFMANN ALBUMS IN THE U.S. NATIONAL ARCHIVES, COLLEGE PARK, MD

Balbo (left) greets Goebbels (right) outside an aircraft hangar. Both Balbo and Goebbels were superb political showmen and on occasion used the public funerals of slain party members to gain political sympathy for their respective causes. PREVIOUSLY UNPUBLISHED PHOTO FROM THE HEINRICH HOFFMANN ALBUMS IN THE U.S. NATIONAL ARCHIVES, COLLEGE PARK, MD

Balbo Reigns as Governor General of Italian Libya, 1934-40

"Totalitarian political theory harmonized with his natural impulses, his drive to be everywhere, to do and control everything."
—Claudio Segrè, writing of Italo Balbo

By the year 1932—a decade after the March on Rome—Italo Balbo had become a serious thorn in the Duce's side. The following episode, included by Jack Gourlay in his book, *Mussolini: A Biography*, reveals the animosity between the Duce and his air marshal. "The 'no smoking' sign went up in the meeting room of the Grand Council in Palazzo Venizia, causing Balbo to object that he, De Bono, De Vecchi, Biancchi and Mussolini had been 'blowing smoke at each other for years.'"

Partly in anger at such lese majesty, the following year the Duce appointed Balbo Governor General of Libya. Then, as if to underscore the air marshal's political exile from Rome, the Duce purged the air ministry of "Balbisti"—the aviator's supporters. Balbo even had difficulty maintaining a small liaison office in the air ministry building.

Writes Kirkpatrick in *Mussolini: A Study in Power*, "Mussolini was glad to export him [Balbo] from Italy, for he disliked him personally and had little confidence in either his loyalty or his good sense. Having discarded Grandi and Balbo, Mussolini was more than ever in personal control of the machinery of the government."

Yet for all their loathing of the man, the leadership cadre of the Party realized that due to Balbo's immense popularity with the people, the fascist militia and the Royal Italian Armed Forces, they could not merely dispense with him. When Balbo, indignant at being displaced to Libya, almost refused to accept his assignment in Libya, the leaders feared a political crisis for the regime.

"Balbo was deeply wounded by this severe and unexpected blow," recalls Balbo's friend Dino Alfieri, the Italian Ambassador to Berlin, in his memoirs. "His first instinct was to rebel, and he told his friends that he would not go, that he would retire from public life and bide his time, but a few of the most loyal and intelligent among them did their utmost to dissuade him from this course.

"If he refused the post, they said, he would inevitably place his family, his many friends and himself in a difficult and dangerous position. If he accepted it, he would enjoy an interval of peace and comparative repose after a long and intensely active career as an aviator in the course of which he had often kept his wife and young daughters on tenterhooks...Balbo allowed himself to be convinced and reluctantly paid his farewell visit to the Duce. His manner at the outset was as cold as it was correct, but Mussolini—as always when he wanted to win someone over to his side, whether an Italian or a foreigner—was particularly cordial and friendly. And Balbo, a sensitive man in whom Mussolini inspired a genuine loyalty and affection, went away satisfied."

Arriving in Tripoli on January 15, 1934, Balbo sent Mussolini a telegram that read, "I begin my new work with the cry, 'Long live the Duce!" Here Balbo would remain until his death in 1940.

Libya had been taken by Italy in the 1911 war with Turkey. Notes Segrè, "Balbo's new fiefdom was a huge, impoverished, virtually empty territory, nothing like today's oil-rich nation. The colony was slightly larger than the present state, which encompasses 1.8 million square kilometers and ranks as Africa's fourth largest nation. More than ninety percent of the land is desert; the majority of the population huddles along the Mediterranean coast on less than three percent of the country's total area. At Balbo's direction, an Italian geologist made tentative efforts to prospect for oil along the coast and traces were found. However, the Italians had neither the capital nor the technology to explore deep in the Sirte Desert, where the first major strike was made in 1959."

During Balbo's time, the only Libyan export product was farming, a bleak prospect at best. After more than two decades of the Italian presence in-country, there were 50,000 Italian residents, most of them in the capital city of Tripoli.

Asserts Dr. Segrè, "Balbo's mission was...to transform a barren, backward colonial territory into an extension of Italy—a 'fourth shore' to add to Italy's Tyrrhenian, Adriatic, and Sicilian shores. To do this, he had to resolve certain concrete problems: provide for Libya's administrative and physical unity, attract colonists, resolve the colony's economic im-

Balbo (left) gives the Fascist salute during his tenure as Governor General of Libya. States author Richard Collier: "At heart, Balbo was still the impulsive soldier of fortune who had helped organize the March on Rome. Well aware that for five years he had governed Libya as pennance for his plain speaking, he still told Mussolini the truth as he saw it—often, when memos went unanswered, flying in from Tripoli to do just that. Embittered by his 'exile' and the knowledge that newspapers could mention him only once a month, Balbo governed well by fits and starts." LIBRARY OF CONGRESS, WASHINGTON, D.C.

The Villa Busetta was Balbo's palatial residence while Governor General of Libya. PREVIOUSLY UNPUBLISHED PHOTO FROM THE HERMANN GÖRING ALBUMS IN THE LIBRARY OF CONGRESS, WASHINGTON, D.C.

balance and integrate the indigenous Libyans."

Balbo came to the task with several advantages. The country was at peace, the fascist regime in Rome backed him fully, and colonization would ease Italy's unemployment problem. Furthermore, he was the second *quadrumvir* (De Bono the first) and the second marshal (after Badoglio) to serve as governor general.

Balbo ruled from the old Turkish governor's palace in Tripoli, which he had guarded not by Italians but by Libyan colonial troops. Whereas the two previous governors, Marshals Badoglio and Rodolfo Graziani respectively, had fought constantly over territoriality, Balbo unified the separate administrations of Tripolitania and Cyrenaica. This ended with a royal decree from the king on December 3, 1934, a signal victory to cap Balbo's first year in office.

Balbo also improved communications and transit across Libya. "When he first arrived," reports Segrè, "the chief link between Tripolitania and Cyrenaica was, as it had been for twenty years, a weekly boat. Neither roads nor telegraph lines linked the two regions. Communications with the mother country were equally tenuous...Within the first two years of his governorship, Ala Littoria instituted daily flights to Tripoli, and biweekly flights linked Libya with Egypt and East Africa; the telephone network, especially in Tripolitania, nearly tripled in size; and on April 1, 1935, a radio telephone tied Tripoli to Rome.

"These accomplishments did not have the grandeur and visibility of his best-known achievement: the construction of the Litoranea Libica, the 1,822-kilometer coastal highway that stretched from the Tunisian frontier to the Egyptian border. In his honor, the road, which was completed in a little more than a year from 1936 to 1937, became known as the Balbia." Adds Segrè, "Contemporary accounts sometimes imply that Balbo built an entirely new road, but only 799 of the total 1,822 kilometers were entirely new."

Despite Balbo's best efforts, however, the colony was a drain on the Italian economy, not a money-maker, as was the rest of Mussolini's new Roman Empire. Balbo's major goal was to stimulate colonization: to offset the native population of 700,000 he hoped to have 500,000 Italians living in the colony by 1950. Balbo sponsored several efforts to attract colonists including air rallies initiated in 1935. These rallies provided Balbo an opportunity to entertain both the King and the Duce, as well as top German Nazi leaders such as Reichsführer SS Heinrich Himmler, Deputy Führer Rudolf Hess and Luftwaffe Field Marshal Hermann Göring.

According to Segrè, "Like any host who loves to entertain, Balbo took great pains to make his home and capital city attractive. 'Tripoli was a jewel personally carved by Italo Balbo...He had built nearly everything in it and built well,' the English journalist G. L. Steer wrote of his visit to Libya in 1938. Others described it as the 'Cannes of North Africa,' or as 'resembling a city in Florida or in Southern California,' or as 'better than the French Riviera.'"

Concludes Segrè, "Balbo could claim much of the credit for this metamorphosis." Additionally, Balbo took a personal interest in the excavation of ancient historical sites and ruins, as well as the Tripoli Grand Prix auto race.

"In the spring of 1937, Mussolini paid a ten-day visit to Libya," continues Segrè. "The occasion was the inauguration of the newly completed Litoranea. The trip had three purposes. First, with the conquest of Ethiopia nominally complete, Mussolini wanted to declare to the great powers his peaceful intentions...Second, Mussolini wanted to make a gesture toward the Libyans. He proclaimed himself as the 'protector of Islam' and thanked the Libyans for their loyalty and support during the Ethiopian campaign...many Libyans had fought in the Italian ranks and contributed to the victory. Finally, Mussolini intended to pay tribute to Balbo. For three years he had worked in comparative obscurity. His 'exile,' some thought, was backfiring on the Duce, winning Balbo support for the development of an anti-Mussolini *fronde*...

For a host in a backward and thinly-populated land, Balbo found an amazing number of events to occupy his guest. There were inaugural ceremonies, military spectacles, theater performances, banquets, horseback rides, and inspection tours of everything from the newly excavated archaeological sites to the colonist villages...On March 15, as Mussolini motored along the road toward Tripoli, Balbo prepared one of his 'pièces de résistance:' the inauguration of the Arae Philenorum, the triumphal arch that marked the boundary between Cyrenaica and Tripolitania. There, in the midst of the Sirte Desert, 320 dusty miles from Benghazi, stood a huge triumphal arch made of Travertine marble, brought piece by piece from quarries near Rome...Balbo arranged for a Hollywood-style premiere. As dusk fell over the

Rivals? The Duce (center) and Balbo (right of center) proudly straddle their horses during Mussolini's tour of Italian Libya in March 1937. At Mussolini's side is the fabled Sword of Islam. The Arabs leading the processional each carry a bundle of rods known as fasces, a symbol of authority in both the ancient Roman Empire and Fascist Italy. PHOTO FROM CAPTURED ENEMY RECORDS IN THE U.S. NATIONAL ARCHIVES, COLLEGE PARK, MD

desert, searchlights lit up the great arch like an altar. Flaming tripods encircled the surrounding piazza. Aircraft rumbled overhead. Honor guards of *zaptie* on camels and a battalion of Libyan soldiers lined the road. Their drumming and piping heralded the arrival of a column of automobiles bearing the Duce and his entourage. To the applause of the Italian and Libyan work crews, the Duce descended from his automobile. 'With his long and sure stride that seems to take possession of whatever land it touches,' Mussolini surveyed the arch. 'Be proud to have left this sign of fascist power in the desert,' he pronounced...

More spectacles followed—this time for the benefit of the Libyans. The following day, March 16, Mussolini made a grand entry into Tripoli. Just outside the city walls, his motorcade stopped. Mussolini mounted a horse and entered the city leading 2,000 Libyan horsemen. Two Libyans bearing huge papier-mâché fasces preceded him like

lictors. He inaugurated the Tripoli trade fair and gave a major speech promising peace and justice to the Libyans and praising Balbo's 'tireless, genial and tenacious' activity as governor. On March 18 came the crowning ceremony: Mussolini received a gleaming 'Sword of Islam' (actually the work of Florentine craftsmen), as a symbol of his role as 'protector of Islam' and successor to the caliph. Anti-fascists and scholars of Islamic affairs snickered at the spectacle and at Mussolini's pretensions. The Libyans did not seem to mind. 'The Oriental dearly loves a show and this was the pomp and splendor of Imperial Rome recaptured for his delectation'; with the Moslems of Tripoli, Mussolini's visit was an 'undoubted' success, wrote an English correspondent...

Personal triumph, return to the limelight: for Balbo, Mussolini's visit was all that, but it also marked a turning point in his plans for the colony's future. With the conquest of Ethiopia, Libya had become a bastion of empire, a center for radiating

Fascist Eagle

SS Reichsführer Heinrich Himmler in Libya

November 1937: German Reichsführer (National Leader) Heinrich Himmler (left, in civilian clothes) visits Libya. German interpreter Eugen Dollmann made these observations: "I believe that Balbo likes me, possibly because of our mutual dislike of Galeazzo Ciano. When the prospect of a Mediterranean war began to make him increasingly apprehensive about the safety of the North African domain to which he had been semi-exiled as a result of petty Roman jealousies, I advised him to invite one of the leading figures of the Third Reich to pay him a visit. His choice fell on Heinrich Himmler, who happened to be visiting Sicily...with his wife...Italo Balbo did his best to entertain them with big receptions, a tour of the souks and an Arab fantasia...Heinrich Himmler was in his element. He could not wear uniform because this would have marred the unofficial image of his lightning visit, but he was able to inspect troops and take the salute garbed in a frightful sports suit and long stockings. His host delighted him still further by conducting a war game on a map table in the Governor's Palace. Balbo...was determined to show that, in the event of military embroilment with England, the game would be lost from the outset. It could only be a matter of time before the whole of Libya and the even less defensible Abyssinian Empire fell prey to the British. With prophetic accuracy, he stressed the difficulty of keeping troops supplied from the other side of the Mediterranean...Himmler flew off in a thoughtful frame of mind. He was delighted with his newfound friend and determined to secure him a cordial invitation to Germany." (Himmler successfully encouraged Göring and Hitler to invite Balbo to Germany the following August.) PHOTO FROM THE HEINRICH HOFFMANN ALBUMS IN THE U.S. NATIONAL ARCHIVES, COLLEGE PARK, MD

Nazi Deputy Führer Rudolf Hess in Libya

Wearing civilian suit and tie, Nazi Deputy Führer Rudolf Hess (center) is greeted by Balbo (left) on a visit to Tripoli. Hess was born in Alexandria, Egypt. On May 10, 1941, nearly a year after Balbo's death, he made his celebrated peace flight to Scotland. Hess died due to questionable circumstances in Spandau Prison in Berlin under British guard on August 17, 1987. He was 93. Hess (right) and Balbo stand at attention during official welcoming ceremonies. Hess straddles a camel for a trip in the Libyan desert. PREVIOUSLY UNPUBLISHED PHOTOS FROM THE HEINRICH HOFFMANN ALBUMS IN THE U.S. NATIONAL ARCHIVES, COLLEGE PARK, MD

Italian power and influence throughout the Mediterranean. Mussolini's trip," concludes Segrè, "was a signal for Balbo to realize his grandiose plans for intensive colonization and to carry out the final legal steps that would create the 'fourth shore.'"

On October 30, 1938, Balbo brought 20,000 colonists to Libya in a mass convoy: "The convoy sailed from Genoa to rendezvous with the six ships in Naples," writes Segrè. "In a final salute to Duce and country, Mussolini, at Balbo's prodding, reviewed the entire convoy before it sailed for Tripoli. With a showman's instincts and an eye on the morning's headlines, Balbo proposed two alternatives: an inspection at anchor off the coast of Gaeta, or one in motion. 'The inspection in motion of a fleet of colonists represents a naval event without precedent,' Balbo informed Mussolini, and the Duce, predictably, favored that plan. With the sea calm and the sun shining faintly, Mussolini, aboard the cruiser *Trieste*, escorted by four destroyers, steamed down the long line of ships bearing the colonists, a line that stretched for nearly eleven miles. The *Trieste* passed close enough to their ships that the colonists could see the Duce's stocky figure on the bridge, his arm outstretched in the 'Roman' salute. The colonists replied with roars of 'Duce, Duce,' and saluted in return. Balbo, always anxious that his productions should please his major critic, telegraphed Teruzzi, 'Please let me know how the review went and if the Duce was satisfied.'...Two days later, the fleet reached Tripoli."

Segrè relates that once in Libya the spectacle continued. "Balbo and his army of aides were there to lead the colonists into the promised land. Along the broad, palm-fringed, ocean-front promenade they marched to the Piazza del Castello, in front of the Governor's Palace, where they gathered for a welcoming ceremony. It took two hours to assemble them all, a gathering 'more impressive than the oft-repeated gatherings in the Piazza Venezia,' remarked one foreign journalist. A gigantic, black, steel-helmeted head, a thousand times life-size, painted on the white wall of the largest building in the square made everyone feel the Duce's presence. So did the banners and slogans that declared 'Mussolini redeems the earth and establishes cities' and urged the new arrivals to 'Begin your new life by vowing that you will be worthy of Mussolini' and 'Let every colonist be a soldier under the command of Mussolini.'

"In contrast to the belligerent warrior's head and the fascist-style martial slogans, Balbo's welcoming

ceremony was 'strangely humble.' The bands stopped playing. The crowd knelt in prayer. A Franciscan gave the blessing. Then, according to Balbo's wishes—and at his mother's suggestion—the crowd recited the Lord's Prayer. 'We were all crying,' Balbo later told his friends.

"Thousands of Arabs in sand-colored robes had flocked into the piazza to watch the proceedings. Balbo did not neglect them," adds Segrè. "The prayer finished, he mounted a rostrum set beneath the wall of the Turkish fortress. All eyes turned to a shrouded monument at his side. When he pulled a cord, the drapery fell away, revealing a bronze equestrian statue of Mussolini. In its right hand the figure

August 9, 1938: Balbo exchanges pleasantries with Göring (right, holding baton) and Foreign Office interpreter Dr. Paul Schmidt (center, in white) at Staaken Airfield outside Berlin. Balbo's visit was designed to turn him into a proponent of the Rome-Berlin Axis and allay German fears concerning his opposition. <small>PREVIOUSLY UNPUBLISHED PHOTO FROM THE HERMANN GÖRING ALBUMS IN THE LIBRARY OF CONGRESS, WASHINGTON, D.C.</small>

brandished the 'Sword of Islam' that Mussolini had received during his visit in 1937; in the left the figure clutched a scroll, a symbol of Mussolini's pledge to protect the Libyans."

To ensure that his "production" received excellent press, in tireless fashion Balbo personally entertained correspondents from Germany, England, the United States, France, Poland, Switzerland, and even war-torn Spain. "Such a good press irritated Mussolini," relates Segrè. "Officially, the Duce congratulated Balbo for 'being the spirit and organizer of this enterprise that is worthy of the regime.' Privately, according to Ciano's diary, 'The Duce was annoyed at the trumpeting made by Balbo over the sending of the colonists to Libya.' In the future, he wanted them to leave in small detachments.'"

Undaunted, Balbo continued to throw himself into his work, and the repercussions of his efforts were felt for many years. A Libyan writer in 1962 commented that, under Balbo's governorship, Libya reached the highest standard of living it had ever known. Segrè, however, adds this caveat: "The Italian farms flourished, of course, at the expense of the Libyans and their traditional forms of agriculture. For his colonization schemes, Balbo claimed the best land for the Italians...In some cases...Libyans were displaced from their traditional grazing lands...the colonist farms disrupted the tightly integrated system of oasis gardens, dry farming, and pastoral enterprises that made up the traditional forms of agriculture in the area. Once their traditional life styles were disturbed, the Libyans became increasingly attracted to the alternatives that the Italians unwittingly provided: wage labor, and the glamour and excitement of the cities."

"Far more important and attractive to the Libyans than the Italian agricultural schemes were the vast building programs," believes Segrè. "The Litoranea, the construction of the colonization villages, and the new buildings in the urban areas provided thousands of jobs for Libyans. Despite the popular belief in Italy that Italians would build the 'fourth shore,' in practice Libyans did, for their labor was far cheaper and more convenient than metropolitan labor."

Balbo pushed for Libya to be legally recognized as an extension of Italy, and Mussolini concurred. On January 9, 1939, the four coastal provinces of Libya—Tripoli, Misurata, Benghazi and Derna—were made part of Italy's kingdom. Balbo could now take credit for having created the "fourth shore."

Balbo also pushed for full citizenship to be extended to the Libyans. This idea, however, clashed with Mussolini's anti-Semitic policies, and Balbo was dealt only *piccola cittadinanza* ("little citizenship") for the Libyans. As Segrè explains, "Qualified Libyans could now acquire certain rights and privileges—mainly that of joining fascist organizations for Libyans." Balbo had lost on this issue, but nonetheless declared that "of all the European powers, Italy had found the best formula for allowing Moslems to become citizens of a Christian state without 'in the least' losing their personal rights according to the laws of the Koran." When thousands of Libyans requested special citizenship, Balbo proudly distributed the first certificates.

"How the Libyans felt about Balbo is difficult to judge because the evidence is so scant," writes Segrè. "Balbo's relatively benevolent policies, after Graziani's repressions, probably won him a certain amount of good will among the Libyans. Perhaps they admired his lavish spectacles and his manly image, his sense of honor and chivalry. They repaid him in kind. A number of times, when Balbo on some aerial or automobile excursion found himself isolated and defenseless in the desert, local nomads helped him. In at least one case they knew with whom they were dealing. Undoubtedly, the Libyans were grateful for gestures such as saving the Tripolitan flocks during the terrible 1935-1936 drought. At that time, Balbo detailed fifty ships to transport 300,000 animals from Tripolitania to the Cyrenaican highlands. The flocks were then gradually driven back to Tripolitania after Balbo arranged for huge quantities of water to be available along the path of the migration...

"In March 1940, the *New York Times* concluded—as most foreign journalists did—that the Italians were not very popular in Libya...Ironically, after Libya's independence—but before Qaddafi's revolution of 1969—Balbo still enjoyed good press among the Libyans. A brief popular history published for the tenth anniversary of Libya's independence praised the material improvements the Italians had introduced, 'particularly under the governorship of Marshal Balbo.'... At its height, before the war broke out, his Libya was a reflection—as he wanted it to be—of fascist Italy. The swarms of military and militia uniforms, the monumental architecture, the statues of the Duce, and the new colonization projects were all faithful mirrors of the mother country. Balbo ruled over Libya as a benevolent tyrant. Totalitarian political theory harmonized with his natural impulses, his drive to be everywhere, to do and control everything. He put his stamp on everything from the editorials in the Tripoli newspapers to the decoration of the chapels in the colonist villages. Like Ferrara, Libya was his fief."

"Without the war, what would have happened to the 'fourth shore'?" asks Segrè. His answer: "Some have argued that Balbo's programs could have worked. Given time and money, the colonists would have rooted themselves, the Libyans would have been integrated, the colony would have prospered. Such a rosy scenario ignores both the realities of Balbo's day and the post-war history of decolonization. Time was the one factor that was in short supply. Italian Libya was a creature of fascist Italy. Ironically, just as Libya reached the peak of its development as a colony, Mussolini plunged into World War II. Many of the agricultural settlements, especially those in Cyrenaica, were destroyed when the Axis and the Allies chased each other back and forth across Libya and Egypt in three successive campaigns during 1941 and 1942...For a few fleeting years, Balbo had transformed the dream of a 'fourth shore' into a reality. Without him, and especially without the financial support of Mussolini's Italy, the 'fourth shore' quickly foundered and disappeared."

Richard Collier paints this interesting portrait of the air marshal-turned-governor general: "Balbo governed well by fits and starts. At times, seized by the demon of restlessness which had made him Italy's most energetic minister of aviation, he threw himself into the work of colonizing Libya, down to such details as furnishing a box of matches for every new settler's kitchen.

"Then, as reaction, black apathy set in. Night after night, Balbo's legendary dinner parties kept his servants up until the small hours; golden lanterns blazed from the palm trees surrounding the palace, an invisible orchestra played, and red-cloaked Spahis stood immobile against a backdrop of white marble. Aided by brimming champagne glasses, beautiful women and choice cigars, Balbo forgot his loneliness in feudal splendor."

Balbo may have forgotten his loneliness, but he did not forget his political views. Notes Jack Gourlay in *Mussolini, A Biography*, "Even from Libya, his voice carried over the distance to Rome, and Mussolini threatened on several occasions to send him to *confino* [jail], or worse."

Back in Rome, Balbo's many enemies stoked the fires of hatred. The Duce's jealous, vain and pomp-ous son-in-law, Count Galeazzo Ciano, included these accounts in his diary: "I received Medici to talk about his row with Balbo...I advised absolute calm. Even if he is right, he mustn't annoy the Chief!" (August 24, 1937) "Talked to Bocchini...a diatribe against Balbo. Nothing I hadn't heard before." (October 6, 1937) "Bonmartini...hates Balbo with all his heart." (February 3, 1938) "It is interesting to observe how anti-Balbo the Grand Council is. The mere fact that the measure had assumed a Balbian character was enough to produce a solid phalanx of opposition." (October 26, 1938)

After a meeting of the Grand Council on March 12, 1938, the Count entered in his diary: "Balbo expresses fears for Trieste and criticizes the proceedings of the Germans. Naturally, he does this behind the scenes and in whispers. Mussolini speaks out at him. He says: 'If we had eight million Italians on our frontiers [as Hitler had German-speaking Austrians on his] we should do just the same. At least I should. I have, in fact, done it.' He is thinking of the annexation of Fiume."

Three months later, Ciano wrote: "A brief talk with Balbo. Sour and hostile to everything. He spoke ill of the Germans, defended the Jews, attacked Starace...and the business of the Roman salute [which Balbo believed had been copied from the Nazis]." (June 18, 1938) On June 23 Ciano added, "Balbo came with me to the [Foreign] Ministry, where we had a long conversation. In the car he uttered literally these very revealing words: 'There no longer exists a taste for sincerity in Italy.' He is depressed. He thinks of staying in Libya, as he realizes that is still the best solution. Fundamentally, he is a man easily dominated and also easily out-maneuvered."

Another entry in Ciano's diary suggests that Mussolini continued to fear Balbo. "At the Chamber, with the Duce and [Achille] Starace [Party Secretary in the 1930s], we talked about Balbo and mentioned certain instances of his behavior. The Duce hates him. He said he will make him end up where Arpinati is [confined as a political prisoner], but, for that, gossip is not enough—we need an incident, a scandal to catch hold of. I asked Starace whether he had taken the hint. He said he had, and thinks of using Consul-General Giannantoni. I think rather of [Ettore] Muti [an aviator], who is intelligent and reliable and would do admirable to trip up Balbo." (March 18, 1938)

On March 21, 1939, the Duce announced to the Grand Council that he intended to support Hitler's

Balbo's Visit to Nazi Germany
August 9-12, 1938

August 9, 1938: Escorted by seven of his most distinguished transoceanic fliers, Italo Balbo flew to Germany for a five-day visit aboard a three-engine Savoia (seen here). German Eugen Dollmann served as interpreter and describes the scene: "The plump Göring was waiting to greet him, resplendent in summery white. The two men's bemedalled chests gleamed and glittered and their satrap-like personalities harmonized immediately." Standing between the two air marshals is German interpreter Dr. Paul Schmidt; at far left, wearing white civilian suit, is the Italian Ambassador to Berlin, Bernardo Attolico. PREVIOUSLY UNPUBLISHED PHOTO FROM THE HERMANN GÖRING ALBUMS IN THE LIBRARY OF CONGRESS, WASHINGTON, D.C.

Balbo and Göring stride across the air field to review a Luftwaffe honor guard with its commanding officer in tow and Dr. Schmidt at far left. PREVIOUSLY UNPUBLISHED PHOTO FROM THE HERMANN GÖRING ALBUMS IN THE LIBRARY OF CONGRESS, WASHINGTON, D.C.

Balbo snaps a salute as a Luftwaffe honor guard presents arms with rifles and fixed bayonets. At left is Balbo's host, German Air Minister and Field Marshal Hermann Göring. During his visit, Balbo presented Göring with a baton described by the Italian Ambassador to Berlin as "an arabesque creation of silver and turquoise." PREVIOUSLY UNPUBLISHED PHOTO FROM THE HERMANN GÖRING ALBUMS IN THE LIBRARY OF CONGRESS, WASHINGTON, D.C.

An exuberant Balbo salutes Göring's personal staff. PREVIOUSLY UNPUBLISHED PHOTO FROM THE HERMANN GÖRING ALBUMS IN THE LIBRARY OF CONGRESS, WASHINGTON, D.C.

Balbo smiles as he and Göring depart in one of Göring's many Mercedes-Benz. PREVIOUSLY UNPUBLISHED PHOTO FROM THE HERMANN GÖRING ALBUMS IN THE LIBRARY OF CONGRESS, WASHINGTON, D.C.

August 9, 1938: During his stay in Germany Balbo was lionized at the House of Flight in Berlin. For the occasion Balbo wore his white Regia Aeronautica undress tuxedo with the German Pilot/Observer Badge awarded to him by Göring on his right breast pocket. In this photo he is accompanied by German Air Force Gen. Erhard Milch. Count Galeazzo Ciano, Balbo's rival in Italy, reacts to Balbo's jubilant visit to Germany in a diary entry dated August 16, 1938: "Now that his [Balbo's] vanity has been flattered, he talks like the most convinced supporter of the Axis. I gather this from his account–the German air force is very powerful and technically more advanced than ours." PREVIOUSLY UNPUBLISHED PHOTO FROM THE HERMANN GÖRING ALBUMS IN THE LIBRARY OF CONGRESS, WASHINGTON, D.C.

August 10, 1938: Resplendent in their dress whites, (from left) Balbo, Göring, and Schmidt visit Carinhall, Göring's estate outside Berlin. Göring helps Balbo sight a hunting rifle. Interpreter Eugen Dollmann writes that Göring welcomed his guest (at Carinhall) as ''one of the Duce's paladins and the man who has recreated the Italian air force, successfully transforming the Assyrian-looking Balbo into a Ferrarese *condottiere* of the cinquecento, a period when beards such as his were commonplace in his native city!'' PREVIOUSLY UNPUBLISHED PHOTOS FROM THE HERMANN GÖRING ALBUMS IN THE LIBRARY OF CONGRESS, WASHINGTON, D.C.

August 11, 1938: Balbo's itinerary in Germany included an outing to the beach and a sail on Göring's yacht, the *Carin* (named after his late Swedish-born wife). For the occasion Göring wears a white yachting suit, a dirk hanging at his side. Balbo prepares to don a swimsuit. Gen. Erhard Milch (back to camera) sunbathes in the foreground. PHOTOS FROM THE HERMANN GÖRING ALBUMS IN THE LIBRARY OF CONGRESS, WASHINGTON, D.C.

August 12, 1939: Balbo (right center) also visited Göring's hunting lodge on the Schorfheide outside Berlin. Naturally, upon his return to Italy, Balbo reported to the Duce. Dino Alfieri describes the scene: "The official Roman communiqué on Italo Balbo's trip was cool and terse. The Duce received...Balbo, who...described, in particular, the strides made by the German Air Force and the extremely cordial reception accorded him by the Führer, Göring, and officers of the Luftwaffe and other services, and the German population." PREVIOUSLY UNPUBLISHED PHOTOS FROM THE HERMANN GÖRING ALBUMS IN THE LIBRARY OF CONGRESS, WASHINGTON, D.C.

August 13, 1938: Eugen Dollmann (center) interprets for Balbo and Hitler. Later Dollmann wrote: "The Italian air squadron landed safely and in glorious weather on the Obersalzberg...The coffee was, by Italian standards, poor. There were no women present, either...We then adjourned to the famous terrace with its broad Alpine panorama...The meeting, originally intended to be a brief one, dragged on and on. Adolf Hitler's eyes glowed, Italo Balbo's eyes sparkled...Finally, in a grave voice, the Führer said, 'Göring and Himmler have informed me of the Africa problem. We shall win there, too, Excellency, because, unlike the democracies, we have the will to win. Convey my greetings to my friend, your great Duce.'" Photo from the Heinrich Hoffmann albums in the U.S. National Archives, College Park, MD

August 13, 1938: Italo Balbo (right) gives the Fascist salute to German children gathered to see him off at the close of his visit, and Luftwaffe Gen. Erhard Milch beams as the children return the Nazi salute. Count Ciano commented on this trip in his diary on August 16, 1938: "Still in a state of euphoria from his journey, he [Balbo] abandoned his attitude of criticizing everything and everybody, except where [the Duke of] Aosta and the Empire were concerned. Balbo is just a great boy, spoilt, restless, lively, ignorant, and at times potentially tiresome. Not, I think, dangerous, because he has no means of being dangerous." Previously unpublished photo from the Hermann Göring albums in the Library of Congress, Washington, D.C.

Governor General of Italian Libya

recent occupation of Czechoslovakia. Reportedly, Balbo openly accused Mussolini of "licking Germany's boots." The Duce was infuriated: not even the king talked to him like that!

Another of Balbo's powerful enemies within the fascist party in 1938 was its secretary general, the war pilot Roberto Farinacci. A super-fascist, his major bone of contention with Balbo was Balbo's vehement opposition to the Duce's Aryan Manifesto. As Farinacci's biographer, Harry Fornari, notes in his 1970 work, *Mussolini's Gadfly*, "Balbo was the fascist leader the least well-disposed towards Farinacci."

Like Ciano and Starace, Farinacci poured poison into Mussolini's ear about the man they all feared the most. "[In 1940] he called Mussolini's attention to a meeting at Rhodes of the three surviving *quadrumvirs*, Emilio De Bono, Cesare Maria De Vecchi, and Italo Balbo, hinting at the possibility of a conspiracy between them and pointing out that Libya, of which Balbo was governor, was the most crucial spot in the Empire, in case of war," writes Fornari. "Typically, Farinacci saw treason and traitors everywhere."

In Dino Alfieri, the Italian Ambassador to Nazi Germany, however, Balbo had a fan. Alfieri writes in his memoirs, *Dictators Face to Face*:

"I returned to Libya in 1937 as a member of the Duce's suite. Mussolini was responding to a pressing invitation from Balbo, who wanted to show the head of government what had been accomplished during his term of office. He was profoundly impressed, not only by the warmth and magnificence of the demonstrations of which he was the object on his arrival and indeed throughout his stay, but also by the many achievements which he was able to verify at first-hand.

"Little villages had sprung up, interlinked by a network of secondary communications; great new roads had been opened to traffic; schools, hospitals and public buildings had been erected in accordance with modern requirements; vast areas of desert had been reclaimed and now yielded an abundance of splendid crops. The military installation conformed to an organic plan, carefully prepared and perfectly executed with a view to defense and offense alike. The stream of immigrants, now in full spate, constituted a channel of communication through which the life of the Mother Country flowed into the colony and revitalized its nerve centers before returning, stronger and more vigorous than before, to its source.

"Balbo had given fresh proof of his exceptional flair for colonial development. Thanks to his assidu-

ous and intelligent work, the authority of the government was widely recognized and Italy's prestige had greatly increased among the native populations, who were not slow to demonstrate their loyalty and gratitude.

"Both during his visit and after his return to Rome, Mussolini was unstinting in his public eulogies of Balbo, but this—far from intimidating the governor's enemies—helped to excite their secret jealousy and the clandestine struggles and palace intrigues were resumed on an even more virulent scale than before."

If Balbo could accomplish this much in a remote backwater so far distant from Rome, what might the popular ex-air marshal do were he to someday succeed the Duce, either by peaceful means or by a coup? This nagging possibility haunted Mussolini, Ciano, Starace, and others within the party hierarchy.

Balbo's career at the Aeronautica was a mixed record overshadowed by fascist politics and hagiography in its own time, and anti-fascist vituperation and recriminations afterwards. No doubt the facts lie somewhere in between. Yet, clearly, Balbo was exiled not in spite of his success with the Aeronautica, but because of those successes, not to mention the acclaim he generated both in Italy and abroad due to his successful Mediterranean, trans-Alpine, and trans-Atlantic cruises.

Segrè writes in his biography of Balbo: "The ministry's equivocal position toward him today reflects the varied attitudes toward his work and achievements. Judgments have ranged from bombastic praise, under the fascist regime, to denigration or, at best, grudging admiration among contemporary critics. Federzoni, though sympathetic to his friend, summarized the case against Balbo. His contribution was characteristic of so many fascist endeavors: far too superficial, far too hasty in his technical development of the service. Yet he did wonders for the prestige and morale of the Aeronautica. It was *his* because the spirits of the aviators were *his*." Other critics, notes Segrè, are not so charitable. "Balbo placed far too much emphasis on showmanship and prestige, they argue. 'Sporting events' such as record flights and air races, promoted Mussolini's regime, the Aeronautica, and Balbo at the expense of the Aeronautica's development. The result was the Aeronautica's disastrous showing in World War II.

"These judgments contain a measure of truth—but also a good deal of exaggeration. They ignore the world in which Balbo worked, a world where aviation was still in its infancy. The great task of the pioneers was to prove that flying was more than a rich man's sport and that aviation had enormous commercial and military potential. These pioneers struggled against enormous odds to reach the public, to overcome suspicion, fear, indifference. In the military field, the Aeronautica in Italy was like air forces in other nations: unknown and untried, lacking traditions, a second-class service, behind the army and navy. By the end of his term in office, Balbo could justly claim that he had built a service with a sense of esprit, high morale, and purpose. His records, his trophies, his sporting successes all contributed to this and to creating an 'air-minded' Italy.

"Too often, Balbo's critics ignore the means available to him. Italy was a poor country to begin with. Furthermore, for political reasons, at least during the period of Balbo's ministry, Mussolini kept the Aeronautica's budget substantially lower than that of the army and navy. With more funding at his disposal, Balbo might have done more. He made mistakes—for example, he was more interested in planning the next aerial cruise than in the long-term development of the service—but, in general, he did the best he could with what he had. To lay the disasters of World War II on his shoulders is ludicrous. By 1940 Balbo had been out of office for seven years. He was not solely responsible for the muddled doctrine and uncertain techniques that hampered the Aeronautica's performance during the war. There was very little he could have done to compensate for Italy's weak industrial base. If the Aeronautica was not ready technically, the responsibility lay not with him but with his successors."

In conclusion, Segrè hands the blame to the Duce. "Balbo," he writes, "was acutely aware of Italy's weaknesses, opposed the war, and predicted disaster if Italy intervened on the German side. The decision to match the Aeronautica against a far more powerful enemy was Mussolini's."

Göring Visits Balbo in Libya, April 9–13, 1939

April 9, 1939: German Air Minister Hermann Göring salutes onlookers with his baton as he steps ashore in Tripoli. Accompanying Göring is his host, Italo Balbo. PREVIOUSLY UNPUBLISHED PHOTO FROM THE HERMANN GÖRING ALBUMS IN THE LIBRARY OF CONGRESS, WASHINGTON, D.C.

Smiling crowds welcome Göring (in white) as he and Balbo (center) stroll the streets of Tripoli. Although Balbo respected Göring, details of the visit reveal Balbo's abiding distaste for the Aryan Manifesto. "Balbo was promoting the Axis—at least officially," writes Claudio Segrè. "Unofficially, in a series of calculated incidents, he delighted in embarrassing and humiliating his guest. As he often did, Balbo invited a dozen middle class Jews to a dinner at the Governor's Palace. Since the occasion was in his honor, Göring could scarcely miss the point. In a second insult, Balbo included a visit to the Jewish quarter and to the synagogue as part of a tour of Tripoli. Göring contracted a 'diplomatic illness.'" PREVIOUSLY UNPUBLISHED PHOTO FROM THE HERMANN GÖRING ALBUMS IN THE LIBRARY OF CONGRESS, WASHINGTON, D.C.

The two air marshals review an Italian honor guard upon Göring's arrival at Balbo's colonial capital.
PREVIOUSLY UNPUBLISHED PHOTO FROM THE HERMANN GÖRING ALBUMS IN THE LIBRARY OF CONGRESS, WASHINGTON, D.C.

April 10, 1939: Göring (white uniform and cap) tours ruins in Leptis Magna in a rail car emblazoned with the Italian Coat of Arms. PREVIOUSLY UNPUBLISHED PHOTO FROM THE HERMANN GÖRING ALBUMS IN THE LIBRARY OF CONGRESS, WASHINGTON, D.C.

April 12, 1939: Balbo's soldiers used hundreds of sandbags to build an impressive reviewing stand for the desert maneuvers staged outside Tripoli for Göring's benefit. PREVIOUSLY UNPUBLISHED PHOTO FROM THE HERMANN GÖRING ALBUMS IN THE LIBRARY OF CONGRESS, WASHINGTON, D.C.

April 11, 1939: German Luftwaffe Field Marshal Hermann Göring (left) and Libyan Governor General Italo Balbo stand on the sandbag revetment to review Italian maneuvers. Behind them fly the Italian national flag (left) and Balbo's personal pennant (obscured) below; to the right, the Nazi War Flag and Göring's banner as Reich Minister for Air Travel and Luftwaffe Commander-in-Chief below. PREVIOUSLY UNPUBLISHED PHOTO FROM THE HERMANN GÖRING ALBUMS IN THE LIBRARY OF CONGRESS, WASHINGTON, D.C.

Fascist Eagle

April 12, 1939: Balbo's grand review included flyovers by Regia Aeronautica CR.32s and exercises by the Italian infantry. Balbo and Göring can be seen atop the sandbag-fortified reviewing emplacement around which the Arab cavalry mills.
PREVIOUSLY UNPUBLISHED PHOTOS FROM THE HERMANN GÖRING ALBUMS IN THE LIBRARY OF CONGRESS, WASHINGTON, D.C.

April 12, 1939: Italian cavalry and trucks and Balbo's legions pass in review. PREVIOUSLY UNPUBLISHED PHOTOS FROM THE HERMANN GÖRING ALBUMS IN THE LIBRARY OF CONGRESS, WASHINGTON, D.C.

April 12, 1939: Balbo and Göring tour Tripoli in Balbo's convertible. Göring cheerfully responds to the applause of the crowd. PREVIOUSLY UNPUBLISHED PHOTOS FROM THE HERMANN GÖRING ALBUMS IN THE LIBRARY OF CONGRESS, WASHINGTON, D.C.

April 12, 1939: Luftwaffe Commander-in-Chief Hermann Göring salutes passing troops with his field marshal's baton. To Göring's left stands Balbo. On his left breast pocket Balbo wears the German Pilot/Observer's Badge presented to him by Göring on the occasion of his visit to Germany in August 1938. As fellow aviators and air ministers, the two men shared a mutual respect. PREVIOUSLY UNPUBLISHED PHOTO FROM THE HERMANN GÖRING ALBUMS IN THE LIBRARY OF CONGRESS, WASHINGTON, D.C.

April 12, 1939: Colonial cavalry and infantry militia are drawn up for Göring's review. Previously unpublished photos from the Hermann Göring albums in the Library of Congress, Washington, D.C.

April 11, 1939: A colorful Spahi Italian colonial cavalryman/standard bearer stands guard at the foot of the reviewing stand during a parade staged for Göring. Previously unpublished photo from the Hermann Göring albums in the Library of Congress, Washington, D.C.

April 12, 1939: Regia Aeronautica bombers line up on the Castel Benito Airfield outside Tripoli for Göring's inspection. "When Italy entered the war," write Enzo Angelucci and Paolo Matricardi, "The strength of its air force amounted to 3,296 aircraft...distributed in Italy itself, the Aegean area, and in Libya. Of these, only 1,796 were ready for action, and these consisted of 783 bombers, 594 fighters, 268 observers, and 151 reconnaissance aircraft. Although adequate from the point of view of quantity, the same could not be said of the force's quality, considering that many of the front-line planes, and the fighters in particular, were inferior compared to those of the enemy."

Balbo's World War II Legacy

"The old man [Mussolini] has gone crazy," Balbo reportedly told his friends.
— Laura Fermi

Fascist Air Marshal Italo Balbo voiced strong opposition to all three of the wars Mussolini entered between 1935 and 1940. The wars in Ethiopia, Spain and the Mediterranean as an ally of Nazi Germany, Balbo believed, would bankrupt Italy as well as ultimately bring the demise of the fascist regime. Balbo proved right. Unlike the leaders of the Third Reich — most of whom lived to stand trial at Nuremberg after the war — the majority of the top Italian leaders were either shot by other fascists or executed by Red Partisans after the war.

With the exception of Balbo, however, fascist leadership in 1935 was supportive of Mussolini's decision to go into Ethiopia. The invasion began on October 3. Four months later, according to Harry Fornari in his biography, *Roberto Farinacci: Mussolini's Gadfly*, Farinacci joined an elite bomber squadron led by Count Ciano. Other members of the squadron included Mussolini's two older sons, Vittorio and Bruno, and party secretary General Achille Starace.

In his memoirs published after the Italian victory, Vittorio Mussolini recalls: "I was a little bit messed up in the first days...I understood very little about ceilings, altitude, firing, bombs, piloting [of his Ca.133], etc...[but] was able to avoid being the dead weight of the squadron, and to do everything the others could do."

Thomas M. Coffey, author of *Lion by the Tail*, writes, "Having calculated the probable route and position of the Ethiopian horsemen on the morning of the ninth, Vittorio and his companions decided to approach them from behind in the hope of getting as close as possible before being spotted..." Soon Vittorio and his companions spotted a few thousand horsemen and dove their airplanes at the targets. "I still have in mind," he wrote, "the spectacle of a little group...blooming like a rose when some of my fragmentation bombs fell in their midst. It was great fun."

Coffey tells of another mission on February 16, 1936. This time Vittorio wrote: "[Saw] more than 50,000 defeated troops plodding southward along the routes toward Quoram and Dessie. Today, the planes were not loaded with bombs...they were carrying mustard gas, which they sprayed mercilessly upon the barefooted men below them."

Continues Coffey, "Along the roadsides south from Amba Aradam, the dead and the gassed-but-still-living lay side by side, equally unattended by their panicky, fleeing comrades. As the planes soared in low overhead, they spurted an oily-looking fluid which fell like light rain, causing screams of pain within moments of contacting the skin of the Ethiopians. Those who absorbed heavy or even moderate doses fell quickly by the wayside, clutching their limbs or their faces, gasping for breath as the lethal gas entered their lungs. Those who were sprayed by only a few drops cried out like the others, but kept moving in the hope that they might avoid the next shower as more planes approached.

"For three more days Italian planes sprayed mustard gas and machine gun bullets on the fleeting Ethiopians until the bodies lay in sprawling piles along the route and an estimated 15,000 men had been added to the 6,000 casualties of the Aradam battle...The army of Ras Mulugeta no longer existed." While Vittorio doesn't report dropping mustard gas, he does brag about the fun he had.

In *Mussolini*, Denis Mack Smith tells of Balbo's reaction. "Balbo commented that their leader had forced the war on them without any prior discussion or consultation, and rarely had an enterprise of such scope been staged with such lack of skill, or with such frivolous naiveté. The political, diplomatic, financial and, indeed, even military preparations had been completely inadequate." Balbo's acid conclusion? "If a man is told one hundred times a day that he is a genius, he will eventually believe in his own infallibility."

As a second world war grew imminent, Mussolini's decision-making style did not change. When Hitler invaded Poland on September 1, 1939, Mussolini decided to stay out of the war despite the Pact of Steel signed just the previous May at the Reich Chancellery in Berlin. "Italians," notes Segrè in *Italo Balbo: A Fascist Life*, "greeted the decision with a sigh of relief. As Grandi noted...unlike World War I...this time the Italian people saw neither a just cause nor

Balbo (second from right) gives instructions to his pilots and air staff officers. In the weeks leading up to Balbo's death on June 28, 1940, the prototype of the Reggiane Re.2001 fighter made its debut. Write Enzo Angelucci and Paolo Matricardi: "It was the first of a new generation of interceptors powered by German Daimler-Benz DB 601 engines, built on license by Alfa Romeo. Due to a laborious preparation phase, the fighter did not go into service until December 1941. On June 5, the prototype of the SIAI Marchetti SM.84, a three-engine bomber destined to replace the SM.79, made its maiden flight. A total of 309 were built, although the bomber never equaled its predecessor. It went into service in February 1941." PHOTO FROM *SIGNAL*, COURTESY OF GEORGE PETERSON, NATIONAL CAPITAL HISTORIC SALES, SPRINGFIELD, VA

The research of James Dugan and Laurence Lafore uncovered reports of this conversation between the German Consul General at Naples and Italo Balbo, who, at that time, was Governor of Libya. "This eminent personage [Balbo] exploded with rage at the Duce...he thought the latter had lost all sense of reality and begun in a quite pathological way to think of himself as 'infallible.'...[The war in Ethiopia] Balbo described as a disaster, and the German Ambassador, Ulrich von Hassell [seen here, right, with the Duce] commented in his reports that his remarks 'amount to a criticism such as had certainly never before been uttered by any Fascist leader, especially to a foreigner.'" PREVIOUSLY UNPUBLISHED PHOTO FROM THE HEINRICH HOFFMANN ALBUMS IN THE U.S. NATIONAL ARCHIVES, COLLEGE PARK, MD

August 4, 1936: Göring (center) converses with the Duce's sons, Bruno and Vittorio Mussolini, who had just returned from participating with the 14th Bomber Squadron over Ethiopia. Behind them stands Göring's longtime aide, Dr. Erich Gritzbach. Vittorio's bloodthirsty passion is well-documented by Thomas Coffey: "Twenty-two-year-old Vittorio, on his first combat mission, had led his flight across the Eritrean border, swooping so low over the Takazze River he could see the crocodiles...Unable to find (a bridge), he decided simply to drop his bombs where they would to the most good—into the midst of the town, but he was quite dissatisfied with his work. He later recalled, 'I saw with sorrow, as will happen to me every time I miss a target, that I obtained only meager results, perhaps because I expected huge explosions like the ones you see in American films. These little houses of the Abyssinians give no satisfaction to a bombardier.'" PREVIOUSLY UNPUBLISHED PHOTO FROM THE HERMANN GÖRING ALBUMS IN THE LIBRARY OF CONGRESS, WASHINGTON, D.C.

the necessity for intervention. When Mussolini finally declared war, the people followed 'not with the faith of an army, but with the patient resignation of a herd.'"

"In general, the leadership behaved shamefully," writes Segrè. "A few pro-Nazi fanatics were centered on Farinacci...but the king, the major *gerarchi* [old-line fascist leaders], the heads of the industrial and financial world, the military leadership, and the church all balked at going to war. Most of them knew that Italy's military preparation was bluff. They despised the Axis and they lacked faith in Mussolini. They were not even convinced that the war, as Mussolini predicted, would be quick and easy...Not a single major figure—not one—resigned in protest.

"Balbo did not resign, but neither did he have illusions about the war. It would be a repeat of 1918 and the Germans would lose, he predicted. 'I'll bet my head on it,' he declared in November 1939, and added, in a jab at Mussolini, 'You have to be an elementary schoolteacher and never have been to America not to understand these things.'...

"Short of replacing Mussolini, Balbo explored all avenues against the war...In December, Balbo met with the Pope and also shored up his relations with the monarchy." On December 7, 1939, Balbo went so far as to hint to the Grand Council of "possible diplomatic and perhaps even military support of the French and British."

"At the end of January 1940, in another maneuver against intervention, Balbo met with De Bono and De Vecchi on the island of Rhodes," relates Segrè. "Farinacci, recognizing that with their prestige the three *quadrumvirs* constituted an important anti-war force in the Grand Council, warned Mussolini of a 'plot.' Yet nothing overt came of the encounter at Rhodes, beyond mutual commiseration...Balbo, acutely aware of his vulnerable military position in Libya, complained that the colony was considered a secondary theater and he had nothing to fight with...In February, Balbo briefly explored the possibility of having himself named ambassador to Washington in hopes of bringing American pressure to bear on Mussolini.

"Balbo took care to publicize his anti-war views. With urgency and passion he talked to friends, to diplomats, to reporters...'He ridiculed the idea of the Germans winning the war...'

"Finally, in the campaign against the war, Balbo confronted Mussolini directly...Balbo, determined to impress Mussolini with the low morale of the troops in Libya, collected a file of soldiers' letters home that had been intercepted by the censors. When Mussolini refused to look at the letters, Balbo read some aloud: 'We are forming a battery here, but there aren't any cannons'; 'that swine in Rome [Mussolini] is sending soldiers to the slaughter.'" He met with the Duce twice more to protest the war: on May 31 and June 2, but to no avail; Mussolini had already told Hitler he would come in on June 10, 1940.

"From these last meetings with Mussolini," continues Segrè, "Balbo emerged enraged, but resigned. Everything was at stake: fascism, Italy, his career, his very life—and the odds were hopeless. 'It's all over here, because the madman wants to make war,' he told Annio Bignardi. Italy would last six months; he would die a soldier's death in the war. 'As for the rest of you, there won't be enough lampposts in Piazza Venezia to hang you all,' he declared."

According to Segrè, Balbo—colorful, theatrical and blunt, as usual—described the military situation in Libya if Italy entered the war against the British and French in this way: "'Practically hopeless,' caught between the British in Egypt and French in Tunisia 'like a slice of ham in a sandwich.'"

In light of Mussolini's stance and Balbo's opposition, both Ciano and De Bono found themselves less antagonistic toward Balbo. Noted Ciano in his diary on June 2, 1940, "He [Balbo] is preparing to return to Libya. He has made up his mind to do the best he can, but he does not believe that the war will be quick and easy...He is a soldier and he will fight with energy and determination.'...De Bono commented in his diary for August 16, 1939, 'I wouldn't like to be him—the first to be attacked, and a first French success against us would be deleterious.'...

"A German military observer in May 1940 confirmed Balbo's assessment of morale: 'Everywhere the gloom of an impending war was only too apparent—a war that the people did not desire and for which it saw no reason.'

"The shortages of matériel were equally worrisome to Balbo. Tanks, armored cars, anti-aircraft batteries, anti-tank weapons, trucks, modern aircraft—he lacked them all. His repeated requests for them during the previous fall and winter had had no results...

"His defensive fortifications were in a dismal state. When the war broke out, the structures to defend the Tunisian frontier were in their earliest stages. In 1939, out of about one hundred planned

September 26, 1937, Lalendorf, Germany: Mussolini (left) and Göring (center) study a map relating to Germany's largest post-WWI maneuvers near Mecklenburg, maneuvers that helped convince the Duce to join the Axis Pact. Although Balbo strongly opposed the alliance, as Claudio Segrè explains, "Unless he [Balbo] broke with the regime, there was little he could do to stop Mussolini. Should he give up his position, resign his many offices? Should he risk more, perhaps even his life, by organizing a revolt? Beyond his immediate coterie of faithful, who would have followed him? The other *gerarchi* [elder statesmen], suspicious, mistrustful, jealous, perhaps ready to betray him for the sake of their own advantage? The timid king and the army, who feared civil war? Even if he succeeded in ousting Mussolini, would he have been capable of filling the Duce's shoes, of living up to the larger-than-life image that Mussolini and the Fascist propaganda machine had conjured up?" Previously unpublished photo from the Hermann Göring albums in the Library of Congress, Washington, D.C.

Everyone in the reviewing stand during Hitler's State Visit to Rome in May 1938 seems unhappy! From front left are Mussolini, Hitler and King Victor Emmanuel III. Between the Duce and Führer is German Foreign Minister Joachim von Ribbentrop; to von Ribbentrop's left is his glum Italian counterpart, Count Galeazzo Ciano. Nazi Propanganda Minister Dr. Josef Goebbels stands between Hitler and the King; Nazi Deputy Führer Rudolf Hess stands to his left. At top left is Hess' wife; next to her, von Ribbentrop's. Significantly, Balbo, who ridiculed the Italian *passo romano* (Roman step) imitation of the German goose-step as "the shameful waddle of a drunken duck," stayed in Libya during the Führer's visit. Photo from the Heinrich Hoffmann albums in the U.S. National Archives, College Park, MD

Adolf Hitler and Italian King Victor Emmanuel III shared mutual disdain. Recognizing this fact and hoping that the King could somehow save the country from the increasingly hawkish Duce, Balbo gravitated toward the throne. "When the new Chamber of Fasci assembled in March [1939]," recounts Denis Mack Smith, "its members, no longer Deputies but 'Councilors,' were under strict orders to wear Fascist uniform, but Balbo rebelliously defied the order and ostentatiously wore his Royalist decorations, advising others to follow suit." Actions like this caused many to implicate Mussolini in Balbo's untimely death. PHOTO FROM THE HEINRICH HOFFMANN ALBUMS IN THE U.S. NATIONAL ARCHIVES, COLLEGE PARK, MD

King Victor Emmanuel III (left) and Balbo stand for a military review wearing pith helmets. By the mid-1930s in the face of the Duce's growing megalomania, Balbo was beginning to see the Monarchy as a necessary counterweight to Mussolini's drift toward war at Hitler's side. "When the [Fascist] Chamber of Unions and Corporations was instituted on March 23, 1939," Roman Dabrowski reports, "Mussolini proposed to modify the oath of allegiance by omitting the words swearing fidelity to 'The King's Heirs and successors.'...Balbo, who in the early days of Fascism had been a republican, was indignant at the proposal." PHOTO FROM THE U.S. NATIONAL ARCHIVES, COLLEGE PARK, MD emplacements, seven had been completed and thirteen were under construction...The famous 'Graziani wall,' a barbed-wire fence that stretched from the coast southward for about one hundred kilometers, was equally useless. An enemy tank could break through it or nose it aside...Only Tobruk was a real stronghold...

"Balbo's dilemma also reflected both his own shortcomings as a military leader and the confused state of Italy's military preparedness at the outbreak of the war. That lack of preparedness, in turn reflected the nature of the fascist regime, which all too often substituted bluff for concrete policies and actions. For twenty years, Balbo had served as one of the pillars of this regime. What he had sown for two decades, he was now reaping," concludes Segrè sardonically.

Fornari, too, writes of Mussolini's obstinacy. "Having obtained the king's consent to plunge the country into war, Mussolini decided not to consult the Grand Council, knowing that the *quadrumvirs* Balbo, De Bono and De Vecchi were against going to war on the side of Germany [*quadrumvir* Bianchi was dead] and fearing that other members might join them in their opposition." (Even Foreign Minister Count Galeazzo Ciano, feeling that the Nazis had failed to keep the Italians informed of their plans and actions at every turn, had misgivings about the German alliance.)

By this time, according to Mack Smith, Balbo was even more critical of Mussolini's decisions. "He [the Duce] relished the dramatic impact of telling his colleagues that as soon as war was declared he 'would mount his horse and take over command.' Balbo and De Bono...were not alone in wondering whether he was off his head if he could use such language."

In the late spring of 1940, as the crucial hour of decision approached, Laura Fermi notes: "Balbo...then governor of Libya, is said to have informed the Duce of the sad condition of the troops in Libya, the shortage of supplies, sufficient only for a very short conflict. Mussolini did not heed him. 'The old man has gone crazy,' Balbo reportedly told his friends. 'I talk of military cadres, of materials that I need, and he tells me that he cannot delay his appointment with history!'"

In his book *Duce!*, Richard Collier adds this comment: "From Libya, Balbo had already sent word of cannon dating from Garibaldi's time, mounted precariously on garbage trucks." Reportedly, the Duce persisted in his self-delusions until the very moment war was declared. Sir Ivone Kirkpatrick notes in *Mussolini: A Study in Power,* "On June 2, he [Mussolini] assured Balbo that Italy would not enter the war, and the governor returned to his colony in Libya with the comforting conviction that he would not be called on to make any urgent military preparations."

On June 10, 1940, however, the Duce announced that Fascist Italy would enter World War II at the side of the Third Reich. Ambassador Dino Alfieri and German Foreign Minister Joachim von Ribbentrop made a similar announcement from the balcony of the Italian Embassy in Berlin. The fateful die was cast.

Despite the Regia Aeronautica's stellar interwar reputation, fascist Italy entered WWII with a blunted, already obsolete, aerial weapon. The country had rested on the laurels won during the late 1920s and early 1930s under her colorful air minister, Italo Balbo, and failed to make adequate preparations. Thus, the question remains: was Balbo responsible, at least in part, for Italy's poor showing in the war?

Some historians defend Balbo, arguing that he was not in a position of command during the war (nor during the war in Ethiopia or Spain, they add), and that he died 18 days after Mussolini's declaration of war. But, his critics riposte, the air force he forged was the weapon with which Italy went to war. The questions, therefore, persist: how much was Balbo's responsibility or fault, and what effect, if any, did Balbo's transoceanic cruises have on the war?

Author Henry Adams bluntly calls the Regia Aeronautica "a failure rooted in misleading success." "Italy's Aeronautica entered the war as one of the best-tested and proudest air forces in the world," claims Adams. "For nearly two decades, Italian airmen had been setting distance and speed records and winning international competitions. During the 1930s, Italian planes had bombed and strafed a valiant but ill-equipped Ethiopia into submission, and they had helped tip the balance for Franco in Spain. Yet by 1940 the Italian Air Force was bedeviled by problems—some of them traceable to the successes of the past.

"Italian aviators saw themselves less as soldiers than as audacious acrobats of the air who could fly circles around any rivals. That cocky pride prompted fighter pilots to disdain the less flashy bomber pilots and encouraged bomber pilots to emulate the risky maneuvers of the fighter pilots. In a similar vein, the

Italian engineers who had built a superb 2,500-horsepower engine for racing never succeeded in producing a satisfactory fighter engine half its size.

"One-sided victories in Ethiopia and Spain spoiled the Regia Aeronautica for the reality of doing battle against larger powers with the ability to fight back. As a consequence, both designers and pilots were slow to appreciate the value of adequate armament: Italian fighters typically had just two machine guns, whereas the Allied planes they fought against often carried cannon."

Continues Adams, "Italy boasted 3,300 planes when it entered the war, but only half of them were ready for combat. The little wars of the 1930s had used up spare parts and had left the nation no time to restock. (Italy never did build enough parts; it preferred to invest its production capacity in finished planes that looked good on display, but were often grounded for want of spares.) Success had also tempted Italian designers to rest on their laurels. In 1940 more than half of Italy's fighters were Fiat CR.42 Falcon biplanes, solid but obsolete craft that had little chance against British Spitfires and Hurricanes. The Falcon was so slow, in fact, that it sometimes surprised enemy fliers; on one occasion, a Spitfire overtook a Falcon and, unintentionally, rammed it out of the sky.

"Italy eventually developed some of the war's best planes, including the powerful and innovative P.108B strategic bomber...But its fragmented aircraft industry wasted immense amounts of money and experience dreaming up new designs rather than refining the best of the old ones. Thus Italy produced more than twice as many kinds of bombers and fighters as did Germany, whose simpler air force enjoyed far greater success. In any case, material shortages and Allied bombing raids prevented Italy from building enough of any model, old or new. All told, the Italians manufactured only 12,000 planes during the war, fewer than 40 percent of which survived to the Armistice."

Christopher Shores concurs with Adams. "During the late 1930s, the Regia Aeronautica...appeared to the world to be one of the largest, most efficient and most potent in existence. Many countries had thrilled to the brilliant acrobatics of official Italian fighter aerobatic teams, while the same Fiat CR.32 biplanes used by those teams had proved to be one of the most successful and versatile aircraft of the Spanish Civil War.

"General Italo Balbo had become famous for the long-distance formation flights he had led, and theorist Giulio Douhet had a wide following in every air force in the world for his ideas on tactics in future aerial wars. Italian bombers seemed fast and modern, having also achieved considerable success in Spain, and the country's airmen had enjoyed several opportunities to gain experience of modern aerial conflict. The reality, however, left much to be desired. The minor wars in which the Italians had been involved had in several important spheres caused them to develop their air force in the wrong direction...

"The first real test of Italian aircraft and airmen came in Spain from 1936 onwards. Mussolini was quick to provide support for the Nationalist insurgents, an air legion of substantial strength forming part of this aid from first to last. Many Italian airmen received their baptism of fire over Spain, where they fought with some considerable success.

"Against French and Russian-built fighters, the Fiat CR.32 was more than able to hold its own, while the fast new Savoia SM.79 and Fiat BR.20 bombers proved almost impossible for the Republican fighters to intercept. Older Meridionali Ro.37 army cooperation biplanes and Savoia SM.81 bomber-transports also operated satisfactorily, and with only minimal losses.

"While experience in Spain led the Italians to believe that maneuverability in fighter aircraft was of supreme importance, resulting in their ordering new biplane fighters as late as 1939, their first examples of modern monoplane fighters and attack aircraft with retractable undercarriages and enclosed cockpits were tested operationally in the latter stages of the war. By this time, however, the opposition was so slight that no worthwhile lessons for combat could be learned.

"Only in China, where the Japanese Army Air Force had introduced numbers of Fiat BR.20 medium bombers into service, were Italian aircraft tested under less favorable conditions. Here the unescorted bombers were met by determined fighter interceptions over central Chinese towns, suffering very severe losses to the same types of opposing aircraft as had operated in Spain during the later months of the conflict (Polikarpov I-15bis and I-16 fighters). The lessons so gained did not, apparently, filter back to Italy.

"By 1939 most Regia Aeronautica equipment was due for replacement, but production of new aircraft in sufficient numbers had not been achieved when war broke out in Europe in September...The

Italian aircraft industry faced two major problems at this time. Airframe design capabilities were excellent, and fully up to world standards, but no really suitable power plant had been developed, nor was a really suitable aircraft gun available.

"The only engines in full production were radials of substantially lower power than the new in-line liquid-cooled engines available in Germany, Great Britain, and to a lesser extent, in France and the United States. Worse, no promising prototype was yet in view. Most combat aircraft were fitted with the Breda SAFAT machine gun of 12.7mm caliber as main armament. While the caliber was the same as the highly-successful Browning .50 in. weapon, there the similarity ended.

"Muzzle velocity and rate of fire were poor, and available ammunition relatively ineffective. Most shells were constructed for impact explosion, to rip the fabric off an aircraft. However, most modern aircraft of other nations were now increasingly metal-clad, and thereby not nearly so badly affected by such armament. The bulky Breda gun also had to be mounted in the nose of fighter aircraft at this stage, being too big and too heavy for wing mounting in the light Italian machines.

"This imposed the need for synchronization with the propeller, through the spinning disc of which the gun had to fire. This synchronization further reduced rate of fire, and was also to pose many technical problems in action...

"In Metropolitan Italy, Libya, Sardinia, Rhodes and Albania (which had been annexed without a fight during 1939), the Regia Aeronautica possessed 1,796 aircraft ready for combat, with almost 100 percent replacement facilities available. A further force of 187 aircraft with similar reserve levels were available in the East African territories, but these were almost cut off from intervening by British-held territory."

In their book, *Combat Aircraft of World War II, 1938-39*, Italian authors Enzo Angelucci and Paolo Matricardi, state: "Italian military aviation had virtually been living in the past, conditioned above all by combat experiences carried out in particular circumstances (such as the Ethiopian campaign and the Spanish Civil War) that had provided a false impression of the air force and had hampered its modernization. The latter conflict especially, gave rise to the conviction that the aircraft that had achieved such success in that theater of the war would be equally capable of sustaining the burden of a new world war.

"Consequently, a series of decisions arising from this very same conviction and concerning military and industrial planning led, on the one hand, to the maintaining of many existing production lines beyond reasonable limits and, on the other, to the strengthening of technical manufacturing and operative principles that the next few years would prove to be totally inadequate."

In their 1939-40 volume, these authors add, "Although great improvements were made at a qualitative level, particularly in the fighter sector, from a quantitative point of view progress was not remarkable, as the aeronautical industry was hampered mainly by a shortage of raw materials. In 1940 aeronautical production amounted to 3,257 aircraft, a rate that was to remain practically constant throughout the three years of war, and that was totally incomparable to those of the major powers, both allied and enemy."

In *Italy at War*, writer Henry Adams also addresses the quality of Italy's aircraft. "The Cant Kingfisher had its drawbacks...It carried two 7.7mm and two 12.7mm machine guns but was vulnerable to head-on attack, and neither its fuselage nor its fuel tanks were protected by armor plate. The plane's pilots had to depend upon its speed and its ability to perform well at high altitudes to elude enemy fighters.

"The scarcity of strategic metals in Italy dictated that the Kingfisher be made entirely of wood—a fact that left the plane at a disadvantage in air-to-air combat and lessened its efficiency in extreme climates, where the wood might turn brittle or rot. Nevertheless, some 560 Kingfishers were manufactured, and they saw duty everywhere the Italians fought, from East Africa to the Russian Front.

"The crew of five manned one of the 7.7mm machine guns in the Kingfisher's underbelly, and the two 12.7mm guns in the crowded waist section, one each flanking the radio operator."

Continues Adams, "Italians affectionately named their most successful bomber, the fast and durable SM.79 Sparrowhawk 'Gobbo Maledetto,' 'Damn Hunchback' because of the hump on its fuselage behind the cockpit. The hump housed two 12.7mm machine guns; a gondola under the fuselage held another machine gun and the bombardier.

"The Italians built more Sparrowhawks than any other plane. The 594 Sparrowhawks already flying in 1940 constituted almost two-thirds of Italy's bomber force, and during the war an additional 600 came off the line. These versatile trimotors also made fine assault and reconnaissance planes. One was even turned into a radio-guided flying bomb. In August 1942 it was launched—unsuccessfully—against British warships off the Aegean Coast."

Concludes Adams, "Italy had no aircraft carriers from which to attack enemy shipping. The Sparrowhawk filled that gap as a land-based torpedo bomber. Carrying one or a pair of torpedoes under the fuselage, Sparrowhawks plagued Allied convoys all over the Mediterranean—so effectively that by the end of the war every Sparrowhawk still flying had been assigned to torpedo duty." Indeed, arguing that the Italian Peninsula itself was the best aircraft carrier available, Balbo had lobbied for the build-up of land-based planes rather than the development of aircraft carriers for the Regia Marina (Royal Navy).

Angelucci and Matricardi cover the Sparrowhawk in their 1933-37 volume. "The series of three-engined aircraft launched by SIAI Marchetti with the SM.73 saw its most famous and effective version in the SM.79 model...This aircraft played an extremely important role in World War II, rightly finding a place in the ranks of the immortal protagonists of aviation history.

"The SM.79 was adopted by Italy on all fronts for the duration of the war, and although it had been created as a bomber, its true role became the more aggressive one of torpedo launcher, in which it proved to be insuperable. From October 1936 to June 1943, a good 1,217 of these planes came off the production lines, a quantity that was clearly superior to the production standards of the Italian aeronautical industry of the time.

"The SM.79's origins went back to 1934, when Allessandro Marchetti decided to develop a more modern derivative of the SM.73 transport model and the SM.91 bomber. The design formula remained essentially unchanged (three-engine, low-wing monoplane with wood-and-metal structure and mixed covering), although remarkable improvements and innovations were made. These included more powerful power plants (with a consequent increase in overall performance); improved aerodynamics; and retractable landing gear.

"The prototype had been conceived as an eight-seater commercial aircraft with the aim of participating in the London-Melbourne race, and it made its maiden flight in October 1934, piloted by Adriano Bacula, from Cameri airport in the province of Novara. The aircraft's characteristics proved to be remarkable from the start, especially its velocity, which touched 220 mph (355 km/h) at sea level and over 248.5 mph (400 km/h) at altitude.

"The prototype was not ready in time to take part in the international race, but its preparation went ahead all the same. In the summer of 1935, the original 610 horsepower Piaggio P.IX engines were replaced by 750 horsepower Alfa Romeo engines, and the SM.79's performance improved still further. In September, the prototype broke no fewer than six world speed records: over 625 miles and 1,250 miles (1,000 and 2,000 km) respectively, with loads of 1,100 pound, one ton and two tons (500, 1,000 and 2,000 kg), flying at 242.937 mph (390.971 km/h) and 236.711 mph (380.592 km/h). The military authorities showed an immediate interest and requested a second bomber version of the prototype.

"The SM.79 made its debut in Spain in February 1937, but its racing activity continued despite its use in combat. On August 20-21, 1937, five SM.79Cs (racers) took the first five places in the Istres-Damascus-Paris race, with the winner covering the 3,846 miles (6,190 km) at an average speed of 219.212 mph (352.789 km/h), reaching 263 mph (424 km/h) at times.

"In January 1938, another three SM.79Ts (the trans-Atlantic model) covered the 6,120 miles (9,850 km) from Guidonia, Italy via Dakar to Rio de Janeiro at an average speed of 251 mph (404 km/h). On December 4, a plane powered by 1,000 horsepower Piaggio P.XI engines broke yet another speed record with an average of 293.798 mph (472.825 km/h) over 625 miles (1,000 km) carrying a load of 4,400-pound (2,000 kg).

"One hundred and thirteen aircraft of the two-engine SM.79B version were also produced for export (they were sold to Yugoslavia, Iraq, Rumania and Brazil), while the three-engine variant known as the SM.79III, with improvements and more powerful engines and armament, appeared in 1943.

"At the outbreak of war, 594 SM.79s were in front-line service, and they soon added the role of torpedo launcher to their original one of bomber. In this role, the aircraft remained in service even after the Armistice, in the Air Force of the Italian Social Republic, while after the war the surviving planes served for several years as transport planes and for target towing. The last were scrapped in 1952."

Adams also comments on Italy's fighter planes. "The Fiat CR.42 Falcon was the best—and the last—of the biplane fighter aircraft that had dominated aerial combat since World War I. The single seater had an open cockpit; it was made of the finest light metal and had fabric covering aft and on the wings to reduce its weight and increase its maneuverability.

"'I dived to attack,' recalled a British Spitfire pilot of his first encounter with a Falcon. 'As I opened fire, he half-rolled very tightly and I was completely unable to hold him, so rapid were his maneuvers.' Fortunately, the Falcon was as slow as it was agile; its top speed of 270 mph was about eighty less than that of the Spitfire, and its lightness of weight had been achieved at the expense of protective armor.

"Worst of all, Falcons lacked radar—and, frequently, radios as well. The last drawback struck the Italian aviators as particularly ironic: 'After all,' complained one pilot, 'Marconi was an Italian.' Italy's early monoplane fighters were little better than the biplane Falcon. The Fiat G.50 Arrow and the Macchi MC.200 Thunderbolt were slower than the British Spitfire and lacked the Falcon's maneuverability. One pilot dismissed the Arrow as 'Good for touring, but not for war.'

"The Macchi MC.202 Lightning, introduced in 1941 with a 1,175 horsepower in-line engine built in Germany, was the best Italian fighter to see action in large numbers. It flew in Africa, the Balkans, the Mediterranean and Russia, but not until the Fiat G.55 Centaur and the Macchi MC.205 Greyhound were developed did Italy have fighters fast and well-armed enough, with 20mm cannon, to take on the Allies' best. The Centaur and the Greyhound were just arriving in fighter wings when Italy was knocked out of the war."

Continuing, Adams notes, "The Italians used a variety of patrol planes in trying to keep the Mediterranean 'our sea.' One of the most useful, the Iman Ro.43 floatplane, was an all-metal two-seater biplane that could be launched by catapult from a ship's deck, then retrieved later by crane.

"The big, ungainly-looking Cant Z.501 Seagull flying boat was called 'Mama, help!' reportedly because of the fear it inspired in children who saw it flying low over Italy's beaches. The Seagull was slow and built of wood, but its range of 1,500 miles made it valuable for convoy-escort and antisubmarine runs as well as for reconnaissance missions.

"The Cant Z.506B Heron, a trimotored sea-plane, was faster and better-armed than the Seagull—and was renowned as a rescue plane. From 1940 to 1942, Herons plucked 231 downed airmen from the sea."

"In 1943," continues Adams, "the Italians planned to send a new and more powerful seaplane on a one-way transatlantic mission. Two Cant Z.511s were to fly under U.S. radar and launch human torpedoes against ships in New York harbor, but Allied planes destroyed the craft before they could leave...

"Against the wishes of Adolf Hitler and the advice of his own generals, Benito Mussolini insisted that Italy participate in the Battle of Britain...in September of 1940, 73 Fiat BR.20 Stork medium bombers were based in German-occupied Belgium to join the attack on Southeastern England.

"The Italians soon wished that they had remained at home," reports Adams. "The bomber crews, miserable in the drizzly Belgian climate, had a hard time learning to fly in the equally soupy weather over the English Channel. The Storks themselves were no match for British attack planes and ground defenses; they were slow, under-gunned and cursed with fabric-covered wings that were easily shredded by enemy fire. And their fighter protection was inadequate.

"The results were predictable, and embarrassing. In four months, the Storks flew only two daylight raids and a few night missions. They frequently carried bomb loads of just 1,500 pounds per plane—and those few bombs fell more often in the sea or in coastal marshes than on their targets. In less than 300 hours of flying time, some 20 Storks—more than a quarter of the Italian force—were destroyed."

Adams believes that the SM.82 Kangaroo was one of Italy's best planes. "A trimotored bomber-transport," he writes, "it had a commodious hold for carrying equipment or troops. The craft also boasted two world records for distance and speed, demonstrating that it could make a long hop in a short time.

"The Kangaroo originally was intended to be used only as a transport. The plane's fabric-covered metal fuselage—the wings and tail were made of wood—could carry six tons of cargo, loaded through a pair of large rear doors. A metal floor divided the fuselage into upper and lower compartments, but the floor could be removed to accommodate especially bulky loads. The Kangaroo had space for 40 fully equipped paratroopers, 600 gallons of fuel or—with the floor taken out—a single Fiat CR.42 Falcon with its wings and spare parts stored alongside. In all, the SM.82 transported some 50 Falcons from Italy to air bases in Italian East Africa, a trip the single-engine fighters could not have made under their own power.

"As a heavy bomber, the Kangaroo could carry an equally impressive load—eight 1,100-pound bombs or twenty-seven 220-pounders. With a range of 1,865 miles, the bomber could execute surprise night attacks on British-held cities and ports as far away as Palestine.

"Even the Germans who were generally contemptuous of the Italians' planes, were favorably impressed by the Kangaroo, Adams notes. Almost half of the 875 Kangaroos that the Italians manufactured wound up flying in the Luftwaffe."

Author Christopher Shores, in his 1976 work *Regia Aeronautica: A Pictorial History of the Italian Air Force, 1940-43*, provides more details of Balbo's legacy. "Amongst the bomber units...SM.79s and BR.20s were in service in substantial numbers, while the new Cant Z.1007bis had also reequipped two full Stormi [Wings]. Overseas the SM.81 was still prevalent, though SM.79s had arrived in small numbers in Libya and East Africa.

"In the latter area, however, a large proportion of the aircraft available were still Caproni Ca.133 colonial bomber-transports quite unsuited for modern warfare. The very useful Cant Z.506B maritime patrol bomber floatplane was also in service, but a large number of units still operated Caproni Ghibli and Ca.310 light bomber-reconnaissance aircraft, and army cooperation biplanes. There was a small and somewhat mixed air transport organization, based mainly in Italy.

"Available, too, were three *Gruppi* (Groups) equipped with the latest products of the industry, for which great things were hoped. On the fortified island of Pantelleria 96° Gruppi was based, and flew the Savoia SM.85 twin-engined dive bomber, while in Central Italy and Sardinia were two Gruppi equipped with the Breda BA.88 attack aircraft, also of twin-engined configuration.

"The latter was employed during some of the first actions of the war, the former not at all. Both proved to be total failures, and had to be replaced, the successful German Junkers Ju 87B Stuka being ordered for this purpose."

"Initial fighting over southern France, Corsica and Tunisia was soon followed by the [1940] Armistice which the French grudgingly accepted," notes Shores. "Unable to continue the fight with the Germans, they had no option but to come to terms with Mussolini. Over Libya, Malta and East Africa, however, it was the British Royal Air Force that was engaged and here it soon became clear that a longer conflict was likely.

"So far, the only opposing aircraft that had clearly outclassed the Italian equipment had been the French Dewoitine D.520 fighter. The British at this time had virtually no Hawker Hurricane fighters available in the Middle East, and it was to be several weeks before more than a tiny handful of these had arrived...

"In October 1940, much to Adolf Hitler's annoyance, Mussolini launched an invasion of Greece from his Albanian bases, the Italian units soon being locked in fierce combat with the small Greek Air Force. The British were swift in going to the aid of the Greeks and offered a determined resistance from the start. Soon, RAF Gladiators, Blenheims and Wellingtons were appearing over the front.

"Reinforcements of more modern aircraft had been shipped to the RAF in Egypt and East Africa, the Italians in both areas soon finding themselves up against the formidable and heavily armed Hurricanes in growing numbers. Ground offensives by the British in both these areas around the turn of the year soon had the Italians in trouble, and by early 1941 every front was demanding immediate reinforcements with more modern aircraft.

"Throughout most of 1940, the MC.200 fighters had remained grounded following a series of crashes, but now these were rushed to Albania, and to Sicily to operate over Malta. The legion in Belgium was brought home, more units including G.50bis and BR.20s being dispatched to Libya, while those reinforcements that could make the long flight were sent to East Africa. The newly-arrived Ju 87Bs were also sent to operate over Malta and Greece.

"Furious with the Italians for their handling of the war, and determined to clear his southern flank before his planned attack on Soviet Russia, Hitler decided to send aid to the Italians early in 1941. Elements of the Luftwaffe joined the Regia Aeronautica in Sicily during January for the neutralization of Malta, further units then reaching Libya."

"In April German attacks in Yugoslavia and Greece speedily cleared the British out of the Balkans, whilst Erwin Rommel's first offensive in the Libyan desert rolled them back into Egypt. While the Germans remained in Africa, they soon withdrew from Sicily and the Balkans, leaving these preserves once more to the Italians. Air garrisons were retained by the Regia Aeronautica in Greece and Yugoslavia, mainly for anti-partisan duties."

"As it was now clear that the war was not going to end quickly," states Shores, "arrangements had already been made to acquire manufacturing licenses from Germany for Daimler-Benz in-line engines and Mauser 20mm cannon, in order that new aircraft better able to match their opponents might be built.

"So far it had proved that the CR.42 and G.50bis fighters were superior on most counts to the RAF Gladiator biplane, but inferior to the Hurricane. The CR.42 could be a most dangerous opponent for the Hurricane in a dogfight, but the latter could take and deal out much more punishment, and had the speed to attack and break off combat at will. The MC.200 was in many respects the equal of the Hurricane, though its lack of firepower was critical.

"Generally, the Italian bombers could outrun the Gladiator, but against determined attack by a Hurricane they were all practically helpless. It was abundantly clear that the Regia Aeronautica's most vital need was for an improved fighter aircraft for both air superiority and bomber escort duties. The appearance of the first Curtiss Tomahawk fighters over the Libyan border during June 1941 served to reinforce this need even more.

"Availability of the first examples to reach Italy of the German Daimler-Benz DB 601 in-line engine—of which license production was at once started by Fiat—allowed the aircraft industry to produce new fighter types using this excellent and tested power plant. The successful Macchi MC.200 fighter had already been up-engined in the MC.201 prototype, but availability of the DB 601 resulted in later 1940 in the appearance of the MC.202 Folgore. This proved a delightful aircraft to fly, and also possessed a first-rate performance. It was ordered into production at once.

"Reggiane had produced an acceptable little fighter in 1938, the Re.2000 Falco, but this had failed to gain a major production order. A small batch was produced for the Navy, however, while substantial export orders from Sweden and Hungary were fulfilled. At one point the aircraft was seriously considered for service with the British RAF. With the basic airframe re-engined with a DB 601, this became the Re.2001 Falco II, and was ordered into production, albeit in less quantities than the MC.202. A third aircraft, the Caproni Vizzola F.4, failed to achieve production status."

Continues Shores, "With new fighter equipment on the way, mid-1941 found the Regia Aeronautica heavily involved in North Africa and over Malta while maintaining a substantial garrison force in the Balkan states and the Aegean Islands. The removal of the Luftwaffe contingent from Sicily in spring 1941 left Malta an entirely Italian preserve once more, and regular raids were undertaken throughout the rest of the year by SM.79, Z.1007bis and BR.20 bombers, both by day and night.

"Fighter sweeps and escort missions by CR.42s, and by growing numbers of MC.200s were frequently made, fierce battles being fought with RAF fighters. In the Libyan desert, two British offensives had failed during the spring, the rest of summer and early fall entering a phase of stalemate. During this period, like all forces in the area, the Regia Aeronautica was built up in strength quite considerably. Units of MC.200s, G.50bis and Ju 87Bs took part in regular actions over the front, including some very successful attacks on forward British airfields. Defense of ports and rear areas in Africa was also undertaken almost exclusively by the Italians.

"Meanwhile, Hitler's attack on Russia in June 1941 took the Italians completely by surprise. Eager as ever to be in on the act, Mussolini ordered that an expeditionary force be swiftly assembled and sent to aid the German, Hungarian and Rumanian forces on the southern sector of the front.

"An air element was included, and in August two *Gruppi*, one with MC.200 fighters and the other with Ca.311 reconnaissance bombers, moved to that front, entering action the following month. The first MC.202s to enter service were dispatched to Sicily early in November, proving a most unpleasant surprise for the Hurricanes defending Malta. Their stay was brief, however, for later that same month a major British offensive in Africa began to roll the Axis forces back across Libya. All available MC.202s were at once sent across to Libya to help stop the attack...

"With the British offensive in Africa sweeping all before it, the Germans had once more returned to the Middle East in strength by the end of the year, going initially as before to Sicily, to undertake the neutralization of Malta. This island's ships, submarines and aircraft had been playing havoc with the Axis supply routes to Africa during the second half of 1941. With most Italian units being rushed to Africa, the initial renewed assault of the island was left to the Germans, who at once achieved considerable success

"Supplies began to flow into Africa, and early in 1942 the British advance was halted before Tripoli had been reached. A surprise counterattack by

Rommel's Afrika Korps caught his opponents off balance, and with dangerously extended lines of communication. They were forced back once more, this time half way across the province of Cyrenaica. Here the Axis troops were held, and a line began to form, running inland from the Gazala area.

"Shortage of aviation fuel kept much of the Regia Aeronautica on the ground during the winter of 1941-42, but as the supply situation improved, its aircraft were soon active once more. Already some fighter units had had their CR.42s and G.50bis aircraft fitted with bomb shackles, allowing them to specialize in the growing art of ground attack. With the arrival of increasing numbers of MC.202s, the MC.200s were also fitted for action as fighter-bombers," notes Shores.

Continuing his narrative, he states, "Over Malta the first Spitfires to be engaged in the Mediterranean theater had made their appearance during March 1942, and with the threat in Africa eased for the time being, the Regia Aeronautica once more increased its presence in Sicily to aid the Germans in the attack on the island. May saw the introduction into service over Malta of the first Re.2001s and during the summer these and the MC.202s often proved to be opponents every bit as dangerous as the German Bf 109s for the RAF defenders.

"Italian bombers flew night raids and occasional high-level formation daylight attacks, but at this time the bomber force was playing a less active part in the war generally. A new role had been found for the successful trimotor SM.79 however – that of torpedo bomber. Italian torpedo-bomber crews were to achieve some considerable successes during 1942, gaining adulation in the popular press of a kind reserved for other warring nations for fighter pilots.

"Operating from bases in Sicily and Sardinia, and from the Aegean Islands, they were extremely active against convoys attempting to get supplies through to Malta, both from Gibraltar in the West and Alexandria in the East. Over Africa during 1942, the new MC.202s enjoyed a measure of superiority over the Kittyhawks and Hurricanes by which they were faced, at least so far as general performance was concerned.

"In armament they were still deficient, however, and while later production versions had provision for an additional pair of 7.7mm machine guns in the wings, the main armaments of two nose-mounted 12.7mm Breda SAFATs rarely allowed a skillful pilot to make full use of any positional advantage he had gained during a combat.

"In the summer of 1942, the first Spitfires began appearing over the desert, but initially only in small numbers. These did not at first make too great an impact on the Axis fighters, but other factors began to do so as the year wore on. With the British dug-in at El Alamein from July onwards, Axis lines of communication were long, while the depredation of the Allied forces fathered once more at Malta continued to keep supplies and fuel scarce. By fall, the Regia Aeronautica, which never enjoyed a particularly high rate of serviceability, was making few sorties compared with the established strength available to it..."

During the middle of October, according to Shores, "the final assault on Malta failed dismally, while a few days later the successful British offensive at El Alamein got underway. On November 8, Anglo-American forces landed in French North Africa, and it became necessary to dispatch MC.202s and fighter-bombers to support Luftwaffe units which moved swiftly to Tunisia.

"Other aircraft were moved to Sardinia, from where attacks on the North African ports of Algiers, Bougie and Bone could be undertaken, these having fallen into Allied hands early in the campaign. Re.2001 units were among these moved to Sardinia, flying fighter-bomber missions against Bone, while MC.202s were active over the front which had formed in the mountains just to the west of the main Tunisian city ports of Tunis and Bizerta.

"In both Russia and Libya things were steadily growing worse. By the start of 1943 the Axis forces in the latter area had been driven right across Cyrenaica, and were preparing to face an assault on Tripoli...Many of the units which had been responsible for rear area defense, reconnaissance, ground support, etc. were no longer required, while airfield space was becoming limited.

"Consequently, during January 1943 all units except some equipped with MC.200s and MC.202s were withdrawn from Libya. Tunisia was reinforced at this time with more MC.202s. At Stalingrad the annihilation of the German 6th Army, followed by the collapse of the Rumanian and Italian Armies led the Italian High Command to decide that the time had come to withdraw from the Russian adventure altogether. Consequently, in February the whole Regia Aeronautica element quit the area and this, too, returned to Italy."

Shores continues with this observation: "The new campaign in Tunisia allowed the bomber force to come back to the fore, SM.79s and Z.1007bis trimotors, now joined by the newer SM.84, and by a single unit of...four-engined Piaggio P.108bis, making frequent night raids on the Northern coastal belt. They concentrated particularly on ports and airfields, operating from bases in both Sardinia and Sicily. Losses of these lightly armed and armored aircraft to the formidable Beaufighters of the Allied night defense were to prove heavy, however, and when some units attempted to make anti-shipping raids by day, they rose to unsupportable levels."

"With the entry of American forces into the Mediterranean war, numbers of powerful, four-engined heavy day bombers now began to arrive, B-24s reaching Egypt in limited numbers during summer 1942, while in November B-17s arrived in Algeria. Initially used mainly against African targets, these heavy bombers were available in sufficient strength by early 1943 to begin flying occasional raids on Sicily, and even against southern Italy.

"At first, such attacks were made by unescorted B-24s from Egypt and Libya, but soon these were joined by escorted formations of B-17s from the West. The need for more effective fighters to meet this new threat was absolutely critical, and it was clear that home production alone could not hope to meet this. During 1942 prototypes of improved fighters of the 'Five' series had appeared, making use of the more powerful DB 605A engine, which was also being manufactured under license by Fiat," notes Shores. "The first two of these fighters were the Macchi MC.205V Veltro and the Fiat G.55 Centauro. The former was basically a re-engined MC.202 featuring the same armament, and could be swiftly put into production. The latter—while based on the G.50 airframe—was really a completely redesigned machine, and was a very fine aircraft incorporating a most effective armament of three 20mm Mauser MG 151 cannons and two 12.7mm machine guns.

"To provide more realistic forepower, later production versions of the MC.205V would have the wing 7.7mm guns replaced by MG 151s, experiments having already been undertaken in fitting these weapons in under wing 'gondolas' to a limited number of MC.202s and Re.2001s for anti-bomber work. A complete redesign of the basic Macchi was subsequently produced as the MC.205N Orione. This flew in November 1942, carrying a revised armament of one MG 151 and four 12.7mm Breda SAFATs, all mounted in the fuselage.

"Two months previously, the Reggiane Re.2005 Saggitario had taken the air. Based on the Re.2001, and carrying the same armament as the G.55, this was also an excellent aircraft. All four fighter types were ordered, together with a light fighter, the SIAI 403 Dardo, which incorporated a 750 horsepower Isotta Fraschini Delta in-line engine.

"To guard against shortages of in-line powerplants, a development of the old Re.2000 fighter, the Re.2002 Ariete, had been flown, powered by a Piaggio Turbine-B radial of 1,175 horsepower. This aircraft had also been ordered into limited production during 1942 to re-equip the fighter- bomber and dive-bomber units.

"It was likely, however, to be some time before these new models could become available in sufficient numbers, and in the interim two foreign types were acquired. The Germans supplied Dewoitine D.520s appropriated from the French Army of the Air, and also some Messerschmitt Bf 109Fs. Although intended mainly for advanced training, the elderly D.520 was issued to one unit in Sicily, claims Shores, for anti-bomber operations due mainly to its effective cannon armament and was to prove quite popular with its pilots. The Messerschmitt aircraft also began reequipping a unit for service in Sicily, and were soon joined by numbers of the later Bf 109G variant.

"Attempts to supply the forces in Africa by air at both Tripoli and Tunis resulted in substantial losses of transport aircraft. The diminishing number of airfields left to the Axis in Tunisia and the continual harrying by Allied aircraft, led to the withdrawal, first of the fighter bombers and then of the fighters, until when the last Axis forces surrendered on Cap Bon on May 13, 1943, all air units had already gone.

"Before the final surrender, however, the first production MC.205Vs had gone into action, operating against Allied aircraft from the airfield on the fortified island of Pantelleria, which was situated midway between Sicily and Tunisia. Pantelleria did not remain a base for long; it was neutralized by Allied air attacks during June to such an extent that a subsequent infantry landing was unopposed.

"The full weight of attack was then launched on Sicily, many Allied units moving to Malta for that purpose. The Regia Aeronautica pushed a substantial fighter force into the island to operated alongside the Luftwaffe in its defense. New types employed included MC.205Vs, Re.2005s, Re.2002s, Bf 109Fs and Gs, and D.520s. The preponderance of Allied air power was now so great that a large part of the Axis air force—which enjoyed no proper coordinated air defense control—was smashed on the ground. Those aircraft that got into the air were unable to achieve more than the occasional success, and could in no way make any lasting impression upon events.

"On July 10, 1943, a great invasion of Sicily was launched, backed by a massive armada of shipping. Most bombers had been withdrawn from Sicily, but Re.2002s, MC.200s, G.50bis and Ju 87s were thrown in against the shipping, suffering dreadful losses to defending fighters and antiaircraft guns. At night the bombers from airfields in Italy attempted to strike at the ships also, but were shot down in large numbers by patrolling Mosquitoes and Beaufighters.

"Before July was out, the Axis air forces had been driven from the island, and battered units were desperately trying to reform and reequip on the mainland. In August, Sicily fell, and at the start of September, the British 8th Army invaded the 'toe' of the mainland. Once more Re.2002s and Macchis were thrown in, but with similar lack of success."

States Shores, "Heavy bomber raids on Southern Italy were by now almost daily events, and the surviving operational Italian fighter units, equipped mainly with MC.202s and MC.205Vs, were retained to oppose these. A new Allied invasion was now planned for the western coast of Italy in the Salerno area, Naples being the initial objective. By September 7, the fleets were at sea, but already the Italians had realized that further resistance was hopeless.

"Mussolini had been deposed, and on September 8 an Armistice was agreed. When the American and British troops went ashore the next day, they found themselves opposed only by the Germans. For the Regia Aeronautica, the war was over.

"At the close of hostilities, something over 1,200 operational aircraft of many types were still available in mainland Italy, of which about half were serviceable. Of these, some 500 were fighters, and 300 were bombers. A good proportion of these aircraft were flown south and surrendered to the Allies, while the rest were taken over by the Germans, and the Italian fascist elements who elected to reject the Armistice, and to fight on. Many of the latter aircraft were in Albania, Greece and Yugoslavia, where their use against partisan forces was continued."

This was the disaster Balbo had foreseen and the end of his once proud Regia Aeronautica. His opposition had stemmed primarily from Italy's alliance with Germany. Balbo had visited Great Britain, the United States and Russia; he simply did not believe that Germany and Italy—even with the aid of Japan—could defeat these major powers.

Aircraft of the Regia Aeronautica

The Italian's Cant Z.1007 Alcione (Kingfisher) bomber was described by Henry Adams as "a much better medium bomber than the Stork...Its three 1,000 hp engines gave it a top speed of 275 mph, and it could climb to 13,000 feet in nine and a half minutes—only two-thirds the time the Stork required. The Kingfisher could also carry more than twice the payload of the Stork—up to 4,400 pounds of bombs, or two 1,000-pound aerial torpedoes for anti-shipping missions." Photo from the Caproni Museum Archive, Rome, Italy

"The only example of the Savoia Marchetti S.56 series still in airworthy condition belongs to an American collector... Savoia Marchetti was best known in the 1920s for its large multi-engined flying boats (such as the twin-hulled S.55), but in 1924 unveiled a dainty three-seat type intended for touring and training use... Comparatively small numbers of the family were produced in Italy, including four used by the Regia Aeronautica for training of military pilots." PHOTO BY F. ROBINEAU

Savoia Marchetti SM.79 bombers fly over the Mediterranean in search of the British Navy. Note the interesting juxtaposition of the Fascist emblem (three fasces) on the wings and the crest of the Royal House of Savoy on the tails. The logo on the fuselage sides is that of the 87° Group BT, "Omino Elettrico." PHOTO FROM THE LIBRARY OF CONGRESS, WASHINGTON, D.C.

A Macchi MC.200 Saetta (foreground) and a Fiat CR.32 on the ground in southern Italy. Mario Castoldi designed the Saetta (Lightning) as an all-metal, low-wing monoplane with retractable landing gear and an enclosed cockpit after the Abyssinian campaign made it obvious that the Italians needed a new fighter. The Saetta had a Fiat A.74RC 38 radial engine. Italy entered WWII with about 150 Saettas; total production was 1,153. PHOTO FROM CAPTURED ENEMY RECORDS, U.S. NATIONAL ARCHIVES, COLLEGE PARK, MD

This Macchi MC-202 fighter with "sand and spinach" desert camouflage hangs in the National Air and Space Museum in Washington, D.C. Built in 1941, it had a Daimler-Benz DB 601A-1, 12-cylinder V, liquid-cooled engine of 1,175 hp. Its wingspan was 34 feet, 8-1/2 inches; its length 29 feet, one inch. The plane weighed 6,480 pounds when loaded, and had a maximum speed of 372 mph at 18,050, a ceiling of 37,700 feet, a range of 475 miles, and two machine guns as armament. It accommodated a crew of one. PHOTO BY THE AUTHOR

"An MC.202 Folgiore guided by the men sitting on its wings, taxies on a rough Italian airstrip during the Second World War. The Folgiore was one of Italy's best fighters of that war, and production on a larger scale was prevented only by a shortage of engines." For the MC.202 an imported Daimler-Benz DB 601A inline engine replaced the radial engine in the Macchi MC.200 Saetta, a plane with much agility and ease of handling but whose performance was limited by the comparatively low power and high drag of a radial engine. (Production totaled about 1,100 aircraft. PHOTO BY SALAMANDER

"Seen at the Paris Air Show of 1985, this MC.205V Veltro [Greyhound] had been lovingly restored to pristine condition by Aermacchi...From his MC.200 Saetta with an Italian radial engine, Macchi's very gifted chief designer, Mario Castoldi, developed the MC.202 Folgore... The MC.202 was a good fighter, but would clearly be better still with more power, and as a result the airframe of the MC.202 was married to an imported DB605A engine to create the MC.205 that first flew in April 1942 and revealed outstanding qualities." PHOTO BY M. ROSTAING

February 4, 1942: Mussolini salutes Göring at Furbara Airfield, Italy. Christopher Shores describes the war situation in early 1942: "Over Malta the air fighting was approaching a climax, while in Russia, where a small number of MC.202s had also now been sent, the demands from all fronts were rising, as were losses. At home, occasional night raids by RAF Bomber Command from England against the industrial cities of Northern Italy, caused the retention of interceptor units there as well, while efforts were expended in building up the rudiments of a night fighter force—previously nonexistent in the Regia Aeronautica's ranks." PHOTO FROM THE HERMANN GÖRING ALBUMS IN THE LIBRARY OF CONGRESS, WASHINGTON, D.C.

Italian airmen and soldiers present arms to the Duce and Göring. PREVIOUSLY UNPUBLISHED PHOTO FROM THE HERMANN GÖRING ALBUMS IN THE LIBRARY OF CONGRESS, WASHINGTON, D.C.

In anticipation of Rommel's success in Africa, Mussolini flew to Tripoli with an entourage that filled five transport planes on June 29, 1942. "A white charger awaited Mussolini's triumphant entry, clad in the snow-white uniform of Marshal of the Empire, into Alexandria," writes Richard Collier. "The famous 'Sword of Islam' that Balbo as Governor of Libya had presented him (shown here) was a part of his baggage." When Rommel was beaten soundly by the British 8th Army, Mussolini stalled impatiently for three weeks, then returned to Italy, embarrassed and dejected. PHOTO FROM CAPTURED ENEMY RECORDS IN THE U.S. NATIONAL ARCHIVES, COLLEGE PARK, MD

The Death of Air Marshal Italo Balbo

"Balbo's memory will linger long among Italians because he was, above all, a true Italian, with the great faults and great virtues of our race."
— Count Galeazzo Ciano

The facts of Italo Balbo's death on June 28, 1940 remain mysterious and controversial. "The manner of his death mirrored his way of life: courageous, generous, romantic, but also reckless, despotic, impulsive," summarizes biographer Segrè. "Always one to lead from the front, to set the example, he took off on a self-appointed morale-building mission that exposed him to considerable personal danger. Nevertheless, as his aides protested, the mission was appropriate for Balbo the lieutenant in the *Alpini* or the Blackshirt leader, but not for the air marshal, the governor general of Libya, the commander of Italian forces in North Africa. Moreover, in the past Balbo had shown himself to be a firm believer in military regulations and a careful planner. He had chastised subordinates...for minor infractions of military discipline and had plotted his transatlantic cruises in meticulous detail, yet he embarked on his last flight with remarkable casualness and an impatient disregard for military procedures."

"The precise motivations behind Balbo's last flight will never be known," writes Segrè. "Official versions state that the accident occurred while Balbo was on an inspection and morale-building expedition...Other sources claim that the inspection was only a cover; Balbo's real mission was to hunt more armored cars." (He had captured a British vehicle less than a week before.)

Continues Segrè, "General Felice Porro, head of the Aeronautica in Libya, in a separate aircraft had accompanied Balbo on his last flight. According to Porro, Balbo had been disappointed at the results of his first expedition. His example had not led to the destruction of more enemy vehicles, so he planned a second expedition. The technique remained much the same as on the first attempt. A number of aircraft were to land at Sidi Azeis to act as bait for the enemy cars in the Sollum area. Once the cars had been attracted, a high-flying aircraft would signal for circling Italian fighters and for a column from nearby Ridotta Capuzzo to close the trap...Balbo ordered a rendezvous over Tobruk with an escort of fighters—either three or five, accounts disagree—to accompany him. The fighters might have simply been for protection, since he was venturing into an advanced area. They might also have been useful in his hunting operation...

"The mission was originally scheduled for June 26. However...a violent desert sandstorm made flying impossible for two days. Balbo also received a report that an enemy attack had temporarily closed the airfield at Sidi Azeis. Those on his staff who knew of his intentions...tried to dissuade him."

On the morning of June 28, the weather cleared, and Balbo decided to embark at 3:00 P.M. He assembled his party at Derna. "The number and composition of that party prompted many questions after Balbo's death," writes Segrè. "Why were nine people aboard I-MANU, a standard trimotor SM.79 bomber whose normal complement was five? Why did the party include so many high-ranking officers and so many of Balbo's closest aides, friends, and family?...

"Such questions were natural; yet anyone familiar with Balbo's habits knew that he loved turning such an expedition into 'a sort of family outing.'...The previous week's mission had been similar. On that one, in addition to his normal crew of co-pilot, flight engineer, and radioman, Balbo took along his nephew, a German journalist, a photographer and a cameraman...The entire party, which eventually totaled eighteen, squeezed into two SM.79s...

"The basic crew consisted of Balbo as pilot, Major Ottavio Frailich as co-pilot, Captain Gino Cappannini as flight engineer, and Sergeant-Major Giuseppe Berti as radioman...his nephew Lino and Cino Florio, his brother-in-law. There were now seven aboard, and the engines were turning over. From the cockpit, Balbo looked out and spotted two old friends on the runway seeing him off, Enrico Caretti and Claudio Brunelli...Always a bit of a tyrant, Balbo motioned them aboard...

"About 5:00 P.M., I-MANU, with Balbo at the controls, rumbled down the dusty runway at El Feteyat and took off into the brilliant blue desert sky. Balbo's first checkpoint was the Tobruk-2 (T-2) airfield, about 160 kilometers away. The fighters

When this photo appeared in *Signal*, the German armed forces magazine, the caption read: "Air Marshal Balbo steers his machine himself over the Italian Province of Libya, which has developed enormously in just a few years under his aegis and is now in a most flourishing condition. Italo Balbo, one of the oldest comrades of the Duce and organizer of the Fascist air force, was recently killed on active service in an air combat with British airmen."
PHOTO FROM THE CAPRONI MUSEUM ARCHIVE, ROME, ITALY

Balbo and his men appear elated after capturing a British armored car just after the start of the war in Libya. Barely a week later, on June 28, 1940, the airplane Balbo was piloting was shot down over Tobruk. Balbo and eight of his closest aides, friends, and members of his family were killed.
PHOTO FROM THE CAPRONI MUSEUM ARCHIVE, ROME, ITALY

with which he was scheduled to rendezvous for Sidi Azeis were based there. In the SM.79 trimotor, which had a cruising speed of about 370 km/h, flying time from Derna to T-2 was twenty to twenty-five minutes. Balbo's plane took the lead. Porro followed behind and to the left to watch for enemy aircraft. The route from Derna lay in a southeasterly direction, paralleling the Litoranea as it cut through the rugged limestone massif of the Marmarica. Off to the left, the Gulf of Bomba's blue waters shimmered in the summer sun.

"Before the takeoff, Derna advised T-2 of Balbo's anticipated appearance. The Tobruk airfield received the message; the command post of the naval batteries in the harbor, however, did not. The error was an important one, because command over the anti-aircraft defenses was divided between the navy and the air force. Nor were the naval batteries alerted visually. About two-thirds of the way along Balbo's route lay Ain el-Gazala, the advance warning outpost for the naval batteries. According to regulations, friendly aircraft were required to make a 360-degree turn over the point at an altitude of no more than 300 meters. During those first days of the war, however," Segrè asserts, "the rules were often violated, sometimes through ignorance, sometimes for reasons of inter-service rivalry. The air force, for instance, protested to the navy that for a formation of aircraft to make a full circle was cumbersome and time-consuming. Whether from impatience with these formalities or from eagerness to make up for lost time, Balbo ignored the regulations. He flew at 700 meters...and failed to make a complete circle. Porro, in order to keep up with Balbo, also violated the rules.

"About 60 kilometers from Tobruk, or about seven minutes flying time, with excellent visibility, Porro discerned trouble ahead: 'black clouds of smoke, which I understood to be from bomb explosions at the T-2 airport.' Almost simultaneously he saw...'close to our aircraft the trail of tracer bullets from our anti-aircraft guns.' No one, however, could sight the enemy.

"Porro immediately tried to warn Balbo. He flew very close—there was no voice radio equipment aboard—to Balbo's plane 'to signal to him to fly to the south in order to avoid flying over the field...but despite the signals that both my co-pilot and I made, he saw nothing, because his eyes were fixed on the bombed airfield.'

"What Porro and his flying companions observed...were traces of a British air raid. At Tobruk these were almost a daily affair. On this occasion, beginning at about 5:10 P.M., nine twin-engine Bristol Blenheims, attacking in three waves of three, swooped in suddenly at a low level from the northeast and made a diagonal bombing run over the T-2 airfield. The damage was not very extensive. Most of the bombs fell on the edges of the runway, setting fire to a few of the parked aircraft and a fuel dump. The latter was the source of the black smoke that Porro and the others had observed. What unnerved and infuriated the Italian defenders on the ground were the surprise and the speed of the attack. The first three bombers made their pass before the alarm cannon boomed and disappeared before the Italian batteries got off a shot. The gunners anticipated that this group, which had flown to the southwest, toward the sun, might return for a second pass. By the time the second and third groups of Blenheims attacked, the Italian gunners had recovered enough to fire a few shots, but the enemy bombers veered off unscathed to the southeast toward the airfield at El Adem.

"By about 5:30, when I-MANU and Porro's bomber approached the air space over Tobruk at an altitude of about 1,000 meters, the enemy air raid had ended. The anti-aircraft batteries were silent. Porro, however, sensed danger. Moreover, he had understood that on the way to Sidi Azeis Tobruk was to be only a checkpoint. Yet, to his surprise, Balbo began to descend and Porro 'understood that he wanted to land.' Obediently, Porro intended to throttle his motors and follow Balbo. His young and relatively inexperienced co-pilot, however, instinctively grabbed the stick and gunned the motors to gain altitude. Porro's aircraft climbed well above Balbo's and veered off to the left. His co-pilot's action, Porro reflected afterward, probably saved the lives of everyone on board.

"From the ground, eyewitnesses recall seeing the two SM.79s approaching from the west—from the direction and at roughly the altitude at which the first wave of Blenheims disappeared. Since it was daylight-saving time, the sun was still quite high. 'We saw in the west two aircraft low like the English...even if against the sun their silhouettes appeared confusing, we were convinced that they were two of the three Blenheims from the first wave, coming back for a second pass,' an eyewitness recalled. The tension of the moment and the particular direction—against the sun—from which Balbo's plane was approaching help explain the uncertainty. The poor training of the anti-aircraft crews and their lack of equipment—many, for instance, lacked binoculars—compounded the confusion. Under normal circumstances, the silhouettes of the two aircraft were quite distinctive. The trimotor SM.79 with its 'humped' fuselage and a ventral gondola earned it the unofficial nickname of...'Damned Hunchback.' The British had no trimotors and the twin-engine Blenheim had very different lines. Moreover, Balbo's plane was approaching from the direction of Derna, not from Sollum or Bardia, the normal enemy routes. On the ground, confusion reigned: some swore the British were back; others shouted that the intruders were friendly. The airman in charge of communications at T-2 tried frantically to contact the naval batteries in the harbor and relay the message from Derna that Balbo was expected. He got no answer. During the air raid, his counterparts had abandoned their posts."

Continues Segrè, "The confusion incited one nervous Italian machinegunner, located near the airport, to fire off four or five rounds. He realized his error and ceased fire immediately. The first volley, however, set off the entire anti-aircraft network: 'Everyone was firing: from land, from the cruiser *San Giorgio*, from submarines, from the ships; a real inferno was unleashed around the two aircraft,' a ground observer remembered.

"From the ground an eyewitness noted that Balbo, seeing that he was being fired on, tried to land as quickly as possible. He dove more sharply, at the same time turning to the left. The maneuver merely exposed him better as a target. At an altitude of 200 to 250 meters, with his landing gear down, he was an easy mark. Popular wisdom attributed the fatal shot to a shell from the *San Giorgio*, an old cruiser that had been sunk and heavily ballasted to command the entrance to the harbor. More likely a 20mm incendiary shell from a naval battery located between the harbor and the airfield struck I-MANU's fuel tanks. The big bomber, now in flames, slid over on its left side, crashed on the bank overlooking the harbor, and exploded. Convinced that they had brought down an enemy at last, a raucous cheer went up from some of the anti-aircraft crews.

"Porro...concerned about the safety of his own aircraft, dove sharply for the hulk of the *San Giorgio* to give the impression that he too had been hit...He cleared the harbor...and flew...until he was out of range...Porro flew back to Ain el-Gazala, landed, then sped by car to the scene of the crash.

"The wrecked I-MANU burned fiercely for several hours. Rescue teams reached the scene almost immediately, but the heat, the flames, and periodic explosions of the ammunition made their efforts useless. ..only dental evidence remained to identify Balbo," states Segrè.

The coffins with the remains of Balbo and his comrades lay in state in Balbo's office at the governor's palace for two days; officially, mourning lasted for five. On July 4, Balbo's body was buried outside Tripoli at the Monument of the Fallen. In 1970, when the Libyan government threatened to disinter the Italian cemeteries in Tripoli, Balbo's family brought his remains back to Italy. Balbo now is buried near Orbetello. Curiously, his gravestone bears no epitaph.

Reactions to Balbo's death were mixed, as exemplified in this 1984 account by Anthony Mockler, *Haile Selassie's War: The Italian-Ethiopian Campaign, 1935-1941*: "The Sudanese Herald lined its account of his death with a heavy black border, even though the two nations were at war. Mussolini on the other had did not seem *'eccessivamento adolorato'*—'excessively saddened'—when one of his military staff brought the news to him. Reports Segrè, "Mussolini acted coldly. He gave no commemorative speech...Mussolini's family claimed that he was deeply moved by Balbo's death but that for political reasons, as the 'invincible Duce' leading his nation in war, he could not express his grief. Balbo's friends, naturally, saw matters differently. 'The order is *not to speak of him anymore*,' De Bono noted furiously."

"Göring expressed condolences directly to the widow and attended a solemn mass in Berlin arranged by the Italian embassy," writes Segrè. "Shortly afterwards, he called General Pricolo, Commander of the Aeronautica, to request a souvenir from the I-MANU's wreckage...Pricolo sent him part of the burnt and twisted remains of the flying column. One of the most unusual tributes came from the RAF. In a gesture that recalled the chivalry and brotherhood among airmen during World War I, a British aircraft flew over Italian lines in Libya the day after Balbo's death and dropped a box with tricolored ribbons. The box contained the following message:

"'The British Royal Air Force expresses its sympathy in the death of General Balbo—a leader and gallant aviator, personally known to me, whom fate has placed on the other side.' [signed] Arthur Longmore, Air Officer Commander-in-Chief, British Royal Air Force, Middle East."

Italian army marshal Rudolfo Graziani succeeded Balbo as governor general of Libya. Graziani with a force of 150,000 soldiers held out for only 57 days against a British force of only 36,000. Graziani died peacefully in 1955 at age 73. PHOTO FROM THE U.S. NATIONAL ARCHIVES, COLLEGE PARK, MD

The news of Balbo's death was announced by the Duce's own paper on June 28, 1940. Rumors that the Duce plotted to murder Balbo still persist. PHOTO FROM THE CAPRONI MUSEUM ARCHIVE, ROME, ITALY

The wreckage of Balbo's plane, June 28, 1940. "Stories still circulate today about plots and assassination attempts," writes Claudio Segrè. "Although the details remain obscure, the general outlines of Balbo's death are indisputable. I-MANU and its crew were accidental victims of Italian anti-aircraft batteries." PHOTO FROM THE CAPRONI MUSEUM ARCHIVE, ROME, ITALY

The Duce (left, black uniform) follows the hearse of his son, Bruno, a 23-year-old captain, down the streets of Pisa where Bruno crashed on August 7, 1941. States Henry Adams, "Something switched off inside Mussolini forever. The Duce was proud of his eldest son, Vittorio, 24, who was also a test pilot at Pisa, but the dashing Bruno had been his favorite...Mussolini heard the details of Bruno's death from Vittorio. Bruno had been testing a new bomber, the P.108B, when one of its four engines failed at an altitude of only 300 feet...Thousands lined the roads as Bruno's funeral cortege passed. Mussolini endured the proceedings stoically, but later remarked to an aide, 'I appear calm in front of you because that is how I have to show myself, but inside I am torn with grief.'" Photo from captured enemy records, U.S. National Archives, College Park, MD

At left: A symbolic coffin is draped with the Italian flag at the memorial service for Balbo held in Berlin on July 6, 1940. Göring stands just left of the carpeted aisle, slightly behind the priests. Next to him, in air force uniform, is Dino Alfieri, Balbo's friend and the Italian Ambassador to Berlin. In the book he published in 1954 Alfieri wrote: "As soon as Göring heard the news of his death...and I announced that a memorial service would be held in the Roman Catholic Church of St. Hedwig, he placed the services of the air ministry at my disposal so that the ceremony should prove in every way worthy of the great man who had vanished from our midst. The service was conducted by the Apostolic Nuncio, His Excellency Monsignor Cesare Orsenigo. The...Germans, who were for the most part Protestants, looked on, motionless and sorrowful... The band of the Luftwaffe...began to play Beethoven's *Funeral March*." Previously unpublished photo from the Hermann Göring albums in the Library of Congress, Washington, D.C.

January 12, 1942: Reich Marshal Hermann Göring (back to camera) talks with an Italian air force officer and Italy's Ambassador to Berlin, Dino Alfieri (right) at a reception honoring Göring on his 49th birthday. In his memoirs Alfieri recalls a remark made by Göring following the memorial service held for Balbo at St. Hedwig Cathedral in Berlin. "Göring had followed the various phases of the liturgy with rapt attention. As we were walking towards the door he said to me: 'I cannot understand why that priest—who took so long to put on and take off his ceremonial robes—didn't find an opportunity to mention Balbo's name even once!'" PREVIOUSLY UNPUBLISHED PHOTO FROM THE HERMANN GÖRING ALBUMS IN THE LIBRARY OF CONGRESS, WASHINGTON, D.C.

Duce Benito Mussolini poses in his uniform as Commander of the Fascist Militia. According to biographer Laura Fermi, Mussolini learned of Balbo's death "while on a tour of the French front and did not appear to be moved. [Marshal Pietro] Badoglio, who was with him, comments, 'Perhaps the disappearance of the only one of the Fascist hierarchy who had dared to challenge his supremacy was not altogether unwelcome.'" PHOTO FROM CAPTURED ENEMY RECORDS IN THE U.S. NATIONAL ARCHIVES, COLLEGE PARK, MD

On July 25, 1943, Dino Grandi (left) stunned Mussolini (right) by putting a motion of "no confidence" on the table during a stormy, all night meeting of the Grand Council. On the heels of the bombing of Rome the Fascist regime was facing its crisis. The ghost of Italo Balbo, according to Richard Collier, hovered over the meeting. "Pareschi, a former protégé of Balbo's, made immediately for the Order of the Day lying on Grandi's blotter...'You can say I'm signing for Balbo.'" Deserted by top party officials, the next day Mussolini was fired and arrested by the king. This photo is of a 1939 meeting. PHOTO FROM CAPTURED ENEMY RECORDS, U.S. NATIONAL ARCHIVES, COLLEGE PARK, MD

Fascist Eagle

Most of Balbo's political contemporaries met bad ends. Here, from left, Emilio De Bono, Pareschi, Gottardi, Galeazzo Ciano, and Marinelli (partially hidden by the commander of the firing squad) await execution by fascists of the Salo Republic in Verona on January 10, 1944. PHOTO FROM CAPTURED ENEMY RECORDS, U.S. NATIONAL ARCHIVES, COLLEGE PARK, MD

A Communist firing squad executes Achille Starace, General Secretary of the Fascist Party, in Milan on April 29, 1945. PHOTO FROM CAPTURED ENEMY RECORDS, U.S. NATIONAL ARCHIVES, COLLEGE PARK, MD

Balbo's predictions in 1939 of a grisly end for Fascism proved prophetic. On April 28, 1945, Red Partisans shot and hung Mussolini. He was not given a trial. The day after his death the Duce hangs (far left) with his mistress, Claretta Petacci, and other Fascist leaders. PHOTO COURTESY OF U.S. ARMY SIGNAL CORPS, WASHINGTON, D.C.

Duce and Führer meet at Salzburg, Austria in April 1943. PHOTO COURTESY GEORGE PETERSON, NATIONAL CAPITAL HISTORIC SALES, SPRINGFIELD, VA

In preparation for Hitler's State Visit to Italy, May 2-7, 1938, hundreds of Italian national and German Nazi Party flags are used to decorate building facades in Rome and gigantic "Heil Hitler" and "Duce" banner plaster the sides of buildings along train routes. Fascist color guards line the streets, seen here at the base of a statue of the Duce on horseback.
PHOTOS COURTESY GEORGE PETERSON, NATIONAL CAPITAL HISTORIC SALES, SPRINGFIELD, VA

Hitler attends a naval review held in his honor in May 1938. Top: Dignitaries view the proceeding from a bluff overlooking the Bay of Naples. Bottom: In attendance are, from left, German SS National Leader Heinrich Himmler, Nazi Justice Minister Hans Frank, Nazi Deputy Führer Rudolf Hess, Hitler, unidentified SS man and German Foreign Office official, Mussolini, and Italian leader Dino Alfieri. Middle: From left stand Himmler, German Propaganda Minister Dr. Josef Goebbels, the Duce (back to camera), and Frank. In 1945 Himmler and Goebbels committed suicide, and the Duce was shot. Frank was hanged at Nuremburg in 1946. PHOTOS FROM THE HUGO JAEGER COLLECTION, COURTESY GEORGE PETERSON, NATIONAL CAPITAL HISTORIC SALES, SPRINGFIELD, VA

Writes David Nevin, "An endless stream of flying boats flows between Italian and American flags on this poster announcing Balbo's [North Atlantic] flight. The flight itself was part of an extended celebration—lasting for more than a year—that marked the 10th anniversary of Mussolini's rise to power in Italy." PHOTO FROM THE U.S. NATIONAL ARCHIVES, COLLEGE PARK, MD

"Barely two months after the fall of Addis Ababa (the capital of Ethiopia) in May 1936," writes Claudio Segré, "the Spanish Civil War erupted. Mussolini, drunk with his African victory, intervened massively [on the side of the Franco Nationalists]. 'Crazy,' was Balbo's reaction—or so Farinacci claimed. Even Federzoni admitted that Balbo was 'luke-warm' at best." Raymond Carr adds, "Mussolini's contribu-tion was mainly in airplanes, light tanks and lorries, and ground troops, which at their maximum totaled some 47,000." This booklet published in London attacks Italy's involvement in Spain's internal affairs. FROM THE AUTHOR'S COLLECTION

An Italian Air Force flight suit as it appears today in the National Air and Space Museum of the Smithsonian Institution in Washington, D.C. After Mussolini secured Balbo's resignation from the Aeronautica in late 1933, he "Gave orders to purge the Aeronautica of Balbian influences," asserts Claudio Segré. "'Balbisti' in the Aeronautica were 'suspected and persecuted.' On one of Balbo's first visits to Italy after assuming his position in Tripoli, not a single representative of the Air Ministry was at the train station in Rome to greet him." PREVIOUSLY UNPUBLISHED PHOTO BY THE AUTHOR

The service uniform of the Italian Air Force (Regia Aeronautica) in World War II on display at the National Air and Space Museum of the Smithsonian Institution. States the legend at the upper left, "Maj. Gen. Alberto Briganti, pilot and unit commander in World War II, wore this uniform. His rank is indicated by insignia on both cuffs. Shoulder insignia shows the wearer belongs to the flying branch of the Air Force. The pilot badge is on the left breast over the ribbons for his fourteen decorations and medals spanning both World Wars. They include the Military Order of Savoy, two gold Medals for Military Valor (equivalent of the U.S. Medal of Honor), the War Cross, and the Order of the Crown of Italy. Loaned by Countess Maria Fede Caproni, Armani." PREVIOUSLY UNPUBLISHED PHOTO BY THE AUTHOR

At left: An Italian air crew during World War II. Of Balbo, one American journalist wrote during the training for the 1933 North American aerial cruise, "He seemed to be feared and respected by his men, and at the same time popular with them." PHOTO COURTESY GEORGE PETERSON, NATIONAL CAPITAL HISTORIC SALES, SPRINGFIELD, VA

Index